The
FOLKLORE *of* TREES *and* SHRUBS

ADVANCE PRAISE FOR

The Folklore of Trees and Shrubs

"This is a very enjoyable and educational book. It contains a blend of fact and folklore that makes entertaining reading."

—MIMI WICKLESS, education director
The National Arbor Day Foundation

"More than just folklore, this is an excellent introduction to the human history and economic botany of woody plants. A well-written and useful volume."

—GLENN D. DREYER, director
Connecticut College Arboretum

The
FOLKLORE *of* TREES
and SHRUBS

BY

Laura C. Martin

Chester, Connecticut

Illustrations by Mauro Magellan

Library of Congress Cataloging-in-Publication Data

Martin, Laura C.
    The folklore of trees and shrubs / by Laura C. Martin.—1st ed.
       p. cm.
    Includes index.
    ISBN 1-56440-018-2
    1. Trees—Folklore. 2. Shrubs—Folklore. I. Title.
GR785.M37 1992
398'.368216—dc20   91-42213
                                        CIP

Manufactured in the United States of America
First Edition/First Printing

To my father, Ken Coogle,
who always encouraged me to climb higher

CONTENTS

INTRODUCTION

At the edge of my woods grows an ancient oak tree. Gnarled and twisted, it has withstood the ravages of time and the fury of many storms, but it has not escaped unscathed. Lightning took away most of the tree one spring, and disease and decay have taken their toll as well.

The will to live burns fiercely in this tree. When lightning struck and the tree was reduced to little more than a stump, the life force held strong; fresh, young shoots appeared the next spring and grew quickly. The result is a lopsided combination of old tree and new growth, gnarled branches intertwining with fresh, straight limbs. Although my tree will never win a beauty contest, this tree is a living testimony of an incredible will to live.

We're good friends, my tree and I. It is not the handsome oak that it once was, but its character more than makes up for lost beauty. Asking for nothing from me in return, my tree has offered me shade from the heat of the sun and comfort when I was unhappy. It has been a constant reminder of the life force that flows so strongly in all of nature.

Not all trees are as hardy as my oak. Some species, such as the flowering cherry, are lovely and delicately scented but are fragile and live only a short time. The diversity of tree species on the earth is staggering, and there are trees of every size and shape, color and texture. Each tree offers its own special kind of beauty. To some people nothing is more beautiful than the strange but compelling shape of the Joshua-tree. To others, the soothing symmetry of a Norfolk Island pine is the picture of loveliness. Trees can be grand and majestic like the ancient redwoods, as gnarled and twisted as the olive, as common as an oak or as rare as the Franklinia, a tree seen only twice growing in the wild.

Not only do trees beautify our earth with their rich green leaves and lovely flowers, trees also offer a multitude of riches. For thousands of years trees have provided us with shade and shelter, food and medicine, bed and beauty. From woodchoppers to woodpeckers, an amazing number of living organisms depend on trees for the basis of their existence.

Each tree has a history to tell; each one in its own way is a "tree of life." Some primitive cultures revered trees to such an extent that they actually worshiped many different kinds and attributed to those earthly giants powers and feats of fantastic magnitude. A few species were actually thought to be the source of all life. With their roots firmly planted in the ground, their limbs reaching toward the sky, trees were believed to be that magical link between heaven and earth.

Trees that seem common and unexceptional to us held special promise and mystery to those living in other times and cultures. The common chokecherry was sacred to the Navajo Indians, who made prayer sticks from the wood. Early Christians believed that the laurel would offer protection from sickness and "evil spirits."

According to Greek mythology, the olive was given to mankind by Athena, goddess of peace and war, of the arts, and of wisdom; thus the olive soon became symbolic of peace and honor.

During the nineteenth century, floral symbolism was fashionable in Victorian England. Many flowers and trees were assigned particular meanings. These plants were then sent between friends and lovers, each blossom carrying a different message. (This system of symbolism is known as the language of flowers and is referred to throughout this book).

Not only were trees revered for their magical powers, but for their usefulness as well. Since ancient times, all parts of trees have been used for food and medicine. Parts of the willow tree have been used like aspirin since the first century A.D.. Tea made from the bark of dogwood was used to break fever and stimulate the appetite; and during the Civil War it was used in place of quinine.

Trees were used for cosmetic purposes, too. A cap of walnut hulls was worn to keep hair from turning gray, and if this failed, the leaves of the golden rain tree were used as a black hair dye.

Many delicious and important foods come from trees. Fruits such as apples, oranges, pears, and cherries are of course the best known and best loved, followed by nuts, dates, coconuts, and olives. Some tree foods are not as well known. For example, the bright purplish pink blossoms from the redwood tree are not only edible, they are nutritious and delicious as well.

Trees offer a multitude of uses, and each culture and each civilization has learned to make the most of these living natural resources. Today, however, the world community faces a new challenge in making the best use of the trees that populate our planet. No longer can we cut and take with no thought to the future. The plight of the rain forest is frightening, and the fight to save old forest growth in our own country is no less important.

For the first time in the history of mankind, we must all work together to assure that all humans understand and live according to our role in nature, not as master over our earth, but as part of the living world.

In 1852 Chief Seattle wrote a letter to the United States government in response to its inquiry about buying tribal lands. In this letter he states:

> *Every part of this earth is sacred to my people. Every shining pine needle, every sandy shore, every mist in the dark woods, every meadow, every humming insect. All are holy in the memory and experience of my people. . . .*
>
> *This we know: the earth does not belong to man, man belongs to the earth. All things are connected like the blood that unites us all. Man did not weave the web of life, he is merely a strand in it. Whatever he does to the web, he does to himself. . . .*
>
> *As we are part of the land, you too are part of the land. This earth is precious to us. It is also precious to you. One thing we know: there is only one God. No man, be he Red Man or White Man, can be apart. We are brothers after all.*

As we increase our knowledge of our relationship to the earth, we will better understand how we are a part of the web of life and how we must work together to be good stewards of the natural resources with which we have been blessed.

It is my hope that *The Folklore of Trees and Shrubs* will help us gain a deeper appreciation of the history and personalities of some of the most important plants that green our planet. With increased knowledge and a clearer understanding of the importance of the trees that grow here, we can hardly help but be sensitive and loving stewards of our earth.

The
FOLKLORE *of* TREES *and* SHRUBS

COMMON NAME: *Acacia*

BOTANICAL NAME: *Acacia baileyana*

FAMILY: Leguminosae (Pea)

DESCRIPTION: Covered with small round balls of pale gold flowers in February and March, acacia is a wonderful ornamental tree. It is slender and grows to a height of only 25 to 30 feet. The leaves are blue-gray and are finely dissected. Also called Cootamundra wattle, this species is closely related to green wattle, *A. decurrens,* which is originally from Australia. It is now considered an escape plant in California, as it grows unaided in many parts of the state.

ORIGIN: *A. baileyana* is native to southeastern Australia.

HOW TO GROW: Acacias need full sun and constant moisture. They do best in a warm, dry climate. The trees grow very quickly, sometimes as much as 4 feet per year. The best possible conditions for a good blooming species are cool summer nights and dry winters. *A. baileyana* grows in zone 10. (Two other species, black wattle, which has very dark green shiny leaves, and silver wattle, which has silvery gray leaves, both grow well in southern California.)

A. farnesiana is called *huisache,* or sweet acacia, by Texans. It was thought to have been discovered by Spanish priests in 1611 and then sent to European gardeners. In Italy it was first grown in the gardens of Cardinal Odoardo Farnese, thus the species name. Drawings of the tree were found in a book published by Cardinal Farnese in 1625. By the latter part of the seventeenth century, sweet acacia was found growing in southern France, where gardeners found it much to their liking. "Cassie," as it is called by the French, soon became an important ornamental plant, and the blossoms became an essential ingredient in mixed-flower perfumes. Cassie produces flowers during two seasons, but the most fragrant and useful blossoms are found in September and October.

The wood from this tree is hard, close-grained, and very heavy, weighing 51½ pounds per cubic foot. The heartwood is a rich red-brown color.

A related species, *A. senegal,* is commonly known as gum arabic and is native to northwest Africa, India, and the Middle East. Growing in these arid regions, the tree produces a clear, resinous sap that hardens into small beads 1 to 2 inches across. For centuries the sap has been considered quite valuable. Early Egyptians used it to hold together gems and pieces of colored glass and as a base for paint. Arab physicians used the gum to treat many ailments, thus the name gum arabic.

Traditionally gum arabic was collected by nomadic bedouins. These ancient peoples would make long journeys across barren lands, slashing the bark of the acacia trees on their way. On the return journey they would then gather the large "tears," or beads, of sap that had collected in the open wounds of the tree. Today most of this sap is collected from cultivated trees.

The United States imports more than 11,000 tons of acacia sap annually, most of which is used in the food industry. It gives body and texture to baked goods and is used to create the hard, shiny outer coating found on many candies. Gum arabic is also used by the United States Postal Service in the sweet gummy substance on the backs of postage stamps.

Acacia is the symbol of friendship, and yellow acacia signifies secret love.

COMMON NAME: *Alder, Black*

BOTANICAL NAME: *Alnus glutinosa*

FAMILY: Betulaceae (Birch)

DESCRIPTION: Alders are attractive deciduous shrubs or trees with alternate leaves. The flowers occur in large and conspicuous catkins. Both male and female flowers appear on the same plant. The female flowers develop cones, and both catkins and cones can be found on the plants in fall. *A. glutinosa,* also called European alder, grows to about 80 feet. The rounded leaves are 4 inches long. *A. cordata* (Italian alder) grows to 70 feet. Small branches have a reddish cast, and the 2- to 4-inch leaves are heart-shaped at the bottom. Arizona alder, *A. oblongifolia,* also known as New Mexican alder, grows to a height of 80 feet. It has sawtoothed, oblong leaves and straight, parallel veins on each side; the bark is smooth, dark gray. It is found in New Mexico and Arizona. White alder, or Sierra alder, is a good indicator of water, as it grows only where there are permanent streams. Red alder is considered the leading hardwood in the Pacific Northwest.

ORIGIN: Black alder is native to Corsica and Italy.

HOW TO GROW: Alders are often used in a border where conditions are too wet to support other woody plants. Most alders are hardy and adaptable to a wide range of environmental conditions, withstanding not only wet but also relatively dry conditions. They perform best in full sun. Like members of the legume family, alders have the capacity to fix free nitrogen from the air and put it into the soil in a usable form. European alder grows in zones 3 to 7.

The inner bark of the black alder is considered a natural pesticide. For centuries herbalists have mixed it with vinegar to rub on the body to get rid of lice and mites. The bark and leaves were boiled and used as an astringent or as a substitute for quinine. This concoction was also useful in fighting infection and inflammation.

American Indians used bark tea made from smooth alder to ease the pain of childbirth. It was also thought to be effective in treating

coughs, toothaches, and mouth sores. During the 1800s bark tea was used against syphilis and malaria.

Red alder is used in making furniture, cabinets, tool handles, and pilings. Black alder is highly resistant to decay caused by weather and water and is made into posts and pilings for bridges and sluice gates. The wood was also favored for making wooden shoes in the Netherlands.

The bark of both the red and European alder is used by dyers and tanners, and the wood is useful for smoking meats and fish.

COMMON NAME: *Alder, Oregon*
BOTANICAL NAME: *Alnus rubra*
FAMILY: Betulaceae (Birch)

DESCRIPTION: Oregon alder grows to a height of 40 to 100 feet. It has a straight trunk and thin, rough light gray bark. The buds, which appear in winter, are dark red, opening in spring to reveal male red-stemmed clusters of flowers 4 to 6 inches long. The leaves are 3 to 3½ inches long and about the same width. The tree is also known as red alder because the inner bark is a dark, rich, red color.

ORIGIN: Oregon alder is native from Alaska south along the coast through British Columbia through the coastal areas of Washington, Oregon, and northern California.

HOW TO GROW: Alders need full sun but tolerate some shade. They prefer moist conditions and in nature are almost always found along streams or rivers. In the landscape the trees are useful in massed plantings as a screen or along stream banks to help prevent erosion.

Oregon alder is almost always associated with water, either sea water or mountain streams and rivers, and the trees are often found growing in wet, boggy areas.

The wood is light, weighing about 30 pounds per cubic foot (dry weight). Although close-grained, the wood is soft, weak, and brittle. The heartwood is an attactive light brown color with shades of red.

Even though the wood is not particularly strong, it is harvested and used for many purposes. If it is properly seasoned, it will not warp and is considered highly shock-resistant. It takes paint, stains, and glue easily and is often used for a high-grade veneer. When exposed to the weather, however, it will quickly decay. Oregon alder is used chiefly to make inexpensive furniture such as kitchen chairs. Some unusual uses are for ladder rungs and the inner soles of sport shoes.

Oregon alder is particularly useful in nature, as it comes in quickly after an area has been burned. It grows quickly and soon creates a shady environment for the struggling seedlings of many kinds of hardwood trees.

COMMON NAME: *Almond*
BOTANICAL NAME: *Prunus dulcis*
FAMILY: Rosaceae (Rose)

DESCRIPTION: Almond grows about 30 feet tall and has pink or white blossoms appearing early in spring before the leaves. *P. dulcis* is grown mostly for its economically important nut. Flowering almond, *P. glandulosa,* is more often grown for its ornamental value.

ORIGIN: Almond is native to Western Asia.

HOW TO GROW: Almond needs full sun or partial shade and good, rich garden soil. It can be grown as far north as zone 7.

Almond has been cultivated around the Mediterranean Sea since ancient times. So extensively has it been planted that the original range is not known.

Even in the wild, today's almond is considered a natural ancient hybrid of three wild species found in eastern and central Asia. Almond trees were often mentioned in the Bible. In the Book of Numbers, it is written that the rod of Aaron, placed in the Tabernacle by Moses, brings forth flowers and ripe almonds, signifying God's special commission to the house of Levi.

The Hebrew name for almond is *shaked,* meaning "waker" or "to watch for." To the Jews the almond was a harbinger of spring because it blooms so early in the season. In the Near East, almonds were particularly valued for their oil.

The following legend is told of the origin of the almond:

After the siege of Troy, the Greek hero Demophon was returning home. On his journey he was shipwrecked and was cast upon the shores of a faraway kingdom. Here he was rescued by the king's daughter, with whom he promptly fell in love. He asked her to marry him, asking only that he be allowed to return to his own home to put his affairs in order. He promised to return as quickly as possible. The young girl agreed, and Demophon left but never returned. The girl waited for years and years and finally died of a broken heart. The gods, taking pity on her, changed her into an almond tree.

Flowering almond is a sign of hope according to the English language of flowers. One poet wrote of the almond,

The hope in dreams of a happier hour,
That alights on Misery's brow,
Springs out of the silvery Almond-flower,
That blooms on a leafless bough.

COMMON NAME: *Anise-tree*

BOTANICAL NAME: *Illicium floridanum*

FAMILY: Illiciaceae (Illicium)

DESCRIPTION: Anise-tree has dark green attractive leaves nearly 6 inches across. The flowers are dark reddish maroon and measure 1½ to 2 inches across and appear in spring. The large shrub grows to a height of 10 to 15 feet. Chinese anise-tree (*I. anisatum*) grows to 25 feet. It has thick, fleshy leaves, which are oval and about 4 inches long. The small, fragrant yellow flowers, which appear in spring, are about 1 inch across.

ORIGIN: Anise-tree is indigenous to an area of southeastern United States that stretches from Florida to Louisiana.

HOW TO GROW: Anise-tree prefers rich, moist soil on the acidic side and needs to be grown in full sun or partial shade. It is particularly useful as a large hedge or screen.

Anise-tree is also known as purple anise and Florida anise. It smells somewhat like the true anise, hence its name. True anise was used for centuries as flavoring in soup, liqueurs, and candies. Tea was made by pouring boiling water over crushed seeds. Medicinally the seeds were used to treat problems with the stomach, liver, and kidney.

Star anise, *I. verum*, was also used as flavoring and was found to be of moderate value as a medicine. Chinese folk healers made a tea from the fruit and used it to treat colic and constipation. Distilled oil was used as flavoring for medicine. *I. verum* is the only species in this genus that is not poisonous if taken in great quantities.

I. anisatum, also known as *I. religiosum*, is native to Japan and South Korea. Cut branches from this shrub are commonly used as decoration for graves in the Buddhist temple grounds in Japan.

COMMON NAME: *Apple*

BOTANICAL NAME: *Malus* sp.

FAMILY: Rosaceae (Rose)

DESCRIPTION: Most apples are descendants of *Malus pumila,* the original apple. *Malus sylvestris* is considered a "wild apple" and has naturalized in some parts of the United States. The tree has a rounded crown and a short, stocky trunk. It grows 30 to 40 feet tall. The leaves are 2 to 3 inches long. The pinkish white flowers are showy, the fruit red and tasty.

There are over a thousand varieties of apples available today. These are generally divided into three main groups: 'Delicious', 'Jonathan', and 'McIntosh'. 'Delicious' is by far the most popular and most important economically. It first sprouted in an orchard in Iowa in 1872. 'Jonathan' was first grown in Kingston, New York, and 'McIntosh' came from Ontario, Canada.

Early, midseason, and late varieties of apples can be grown in the home orchard, as can various cultivars suitable for eating, cooking, storing, or making cider.

ORIGIN: Apple is native to Europe and western Asia.

HOW TO GROW: Cultivated apple trees need full sun, rich soil, and plenty of moisture. The best time to plant apples is between mid-fall and early spring. Container-grown trees can be planted any time that the soil can be worked easily. At the time of planting, the soil should neither be frozen nor too wet. Before planting dig a hole large enough to accommodate all the outspread roots and deep enough to cover the top roots with 3 to 4 inches of soil. Stake young trees and water generously.

Apples are considered among the oldest of all cultivated fruits, having been in cultivation since prehistoric times. Today's apple is native to the Caucasus mountains in western Asia. It was brought to England during the time of Roman occupation in the third and fourth centuries.

In Egypt during the thirteenth century B.C., the pharaohs grew apples along the Nile River. In Greece apples were so scarce that by governmental decree a bride and groom could share only a single apple between them on their wedding day.

In time, however, apples became more abun-

dant. By the fourth century B.C., it was written that ladies of the evening in Europe would toss apples to their favorite customers at some of the houses of ill repute. So common was this custom that "tossing the apples" soon became synonymous with sexual intercourse.

Apples were introduced to the New World in 1623. They were brought by an English Episcopalian minister, William Blackstone. Unfortunately, Blackstone's flock did not like the bitterly cold winter of their new country and were fearful of the surrounding Indians, so they soon sailed back to England. Blackstone remained, sur-

rounded by Indians with whom he made friends, and his apple trees, which sprouted and grew but provided little fruit.

Puritans arrived in Massachusetts in 1630, and they also planted apple trees that bore few apples. It was then observed that there were few bees in the orchards. The leaders of the community concluded that perhaps bees in this country were not adept at pollinating English strains of apples. To remedy this they brought over many hives of bees, and the problem was immediately solved.

Apples were soon grown in many parts of the country including the Virginia tidewater area and the southern Appalachians. These delicious fruits were preserved during the winter months by packing them between layers of dry moss in earthen pots sealed with resin. Other means of preserving apples were soon developed. Pennsylvania Dutch farmers peeled and sliced appes and dried them in the sun. They were then hung from attic rafters until used. Extra apples were placed in a big pot and cooked with spices to make apple butter.

Apple cider was not only a delicious drink, it was also the main drink served at social gather-

ings. It is reported that in the late nineteenth century one farmer out of every ten had an apple press.

Perhaps the most famous apple man of all times was Johnny Appleseed, a true-to-life person with an insatiable love of apples. Jonathan Chapman, born on September 26, 1774, was called the "missionary nurseryman" of the American frontier. Johnny Appleseed is said to have looked much like what his name would imply. He had long flowing hair, partially hidden by an inverted pan that he wore to keep the rain off his head. He was usually barefooted, dressed in ragged pants and, for a shirt, an old coffee sack, with holes cut out for his arms and his head. Traveling on foot, he gave away apple seeds to everyone he met; as a result, he is credited with helping to establish apple orchards from Pennsylvania to Illinois. By the time he died in 1845, he owned 1,200 acres of apple trees.

Hundreds of apple varieties have been developed, improving traits such as flavor, color, and high yield. Today the world crop of apples is approximately 47 billion pounds (one quarter of this goes for making cider).

The apple blossom is a symbol of preference.

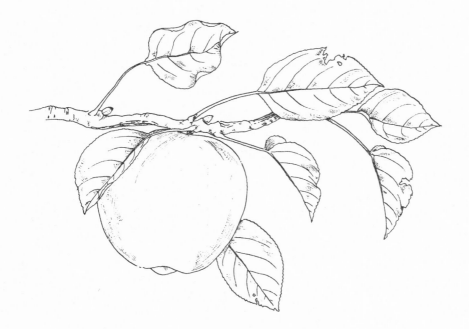

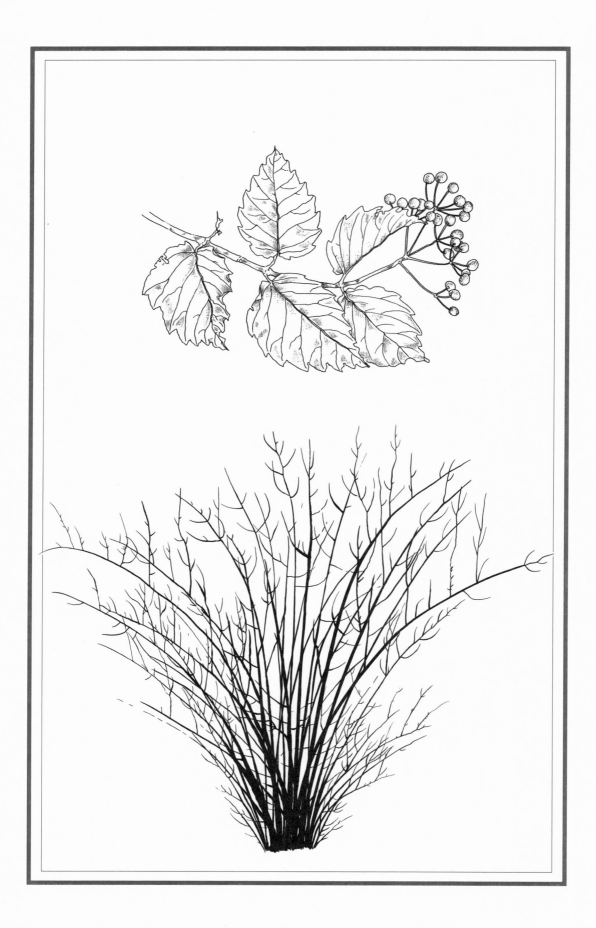

COMMON NAME: *Arrowwood, Southern*
BOTANICAL NAME: *Viburnum dentatum*
FAMILY: Caprifoliaceae (Honeysuckle)

DESCRIPTION: *Viburnum* is a very large genus, grown primarily for its lovely, fragrant blossoms. Some are deciduous, others evergreen. Some bloom during summer, others in fall and winter. *V. dentatum* grows to a height of 3 to 10 feet and has many branches coming from the base. The flowers are white and showy, the fruit a blue-black berry. The leaves are opposite and are ovate (rather than rounded) at the end. The bark is reddish brown and smooth. *V. prunifolium*, blackhaw, grows 30 feet tall and has finely toothed dark green leaves. The fruit is small, occurs in clusters, and turns blue-black when ripe. It is hardy to zone 3. *V. betulifolium* has white flowers in early summer and bright red berries in fall. *V. burkwoodii* has fragrant white flowers that appear from late winter into spring; it is considered semideciduous. *V. davidii* has deep green leathery leaves and a neat, compact growing habit. The flowers are white and occur in clusters in early summer. This viburnum is hardy only to zone 7.

ORIGIN: *V. prunifolium* is native from Connecticut south to Florida and west to Texas. *V. dentatum* is native to most of the eastern United States north of the Florida panhandle to New Brunswick and west to eastern Texas.

HOW TO GROW: Viburnums like to grow in partial shade and tolerate a wide range of soil conditions. Although they are somewhat ordinary looking when they are not blooming, the flowers are so outstanding that they make their inclusion in the garden worthwhile.

Blackhaw is also known as stagbush, sheepberry, nannyberry, and sweet haw. Donald Culross Peattie wrote in *A Natural History of Trees*, "Roadsides and fence rows, dry rocky hillsides and prairie groves are habitats of this bushy understory tree, with its short, crooked, spindling bandy-legged trunk and its graceless rigid branches like widespread arms."

In spite of its "graceless" form, blackhaw does have its attractive points. During autumn the trees turn a brilliant scarlet or burgundy red.

Blackhaw has an edible fruit that was often used by early American folk healers and doctors. It was listed in the *United States Pharmacopeia* from 1882 to 1926.

The poet James Whitcomb Riley wrote, "What is sweeter, after all, than black haws, in early fall?," alluding to the delicious taste of these small fruits.

In 1857 it was written in the *American Family Physician* that fruit from this plant was a "uterine tonic" and that the bark was often used to prevent miscarriages. A concoction made from the bark was also used to lessen the pain after childbirth and to ease menstrual cramps. It was listed as a nerve tonic.

In addition to adventuresome humans, fruits of blackhaw are eaten by gray fox, white-tailed deer, and bobwhites.

COMMON NAME: *Ash, White*
BOTANICAL NAME: *Fraxinus americana*
FAMILY: Oleaceae (Olive)

DESCRIPTION: *F. americana*, white ash, grows to a height of 60 to 120 feet at maturity. Foliage occurs in seven (sometimes five or nine) oval leaflets. The bark is gray and has a diamond-shaped pattern. Clusters of small flowers appear in spring, followed by 1-inch-long winged seeds that stay on the tree until fall. Leaves are dark green in summer, turning orange to purple in autumn.

ORIGIN: White ash is native to the entire eastern portion of the United States (with the exception of Florida south of the panhandle).

HOW TO GROW: Ash grows very quickly and vigorously and is often much stronger than other quick-growing trees. Because of its size and the litter from the seeds, ash is sometimes considered more useful in public grounds (parks, campuses, corporate landscapes) than in the home yard or garden. Seeds self-sow profusely, often creating a maintenance problem. Cultivars have been developed that are male and nonfruiting, making them more desirable for the home landscape. These include 'Autumn Purple' and 'Rosehill'. *F. americana* grows in zones 5 to 9, and some cultivars survive quite well in zones 3 and 4 as well.

In general both the species and cultivars adapt to a wide range of soil conditions if given full sun. Watering during times of drought keeps the trees healthy and vigorous, reducing damage from insects and pests.

Primitive cultures often believed that the tree was the origin of all life. As they saw leaves unfold and branches reach out to form huge trees, they came to believe in a Universal Tree of Life. The choice of the actual "tree of life" worshiped among these cultures depended on which tree grew most profusely within their geographical area.

Because species of ash grew in the great northern forests of Scandinavia, the ash tree was used and revered by ancient Norsemen. The Vikings of Norway and Denmark were sometimes called "Ashemen" because their spear shafts and ax handles were made from this wood. The ash eventually became known as the "great sacred tree of the north."

In Norse mythology a large ash tree named Yggdrasil was believed to be the origin of all life and, due to its size and strength, was believed to hold up the sky. Its leaves were thought to be the clouds and its fruit the stars.

Ash was sometimes used to determine weather. For example, an old English poem says:

If the Oak is out before the Ash,
Twill be a summer of wet and splash
But if the Ash is before the Oak,
Twill be a summer of fire and smoke.

Another English rhyme suggests that green ash wood burns better than any other kind of wood:

Burn Ash-wood green,
'Tis fire for a queen;
Burn Ash-wood sear,
'Twill make a man swear.

Another superstition refers to the European ash, which normally has simple (undivided) leaves. Occasionally a double leaf is found, and this is considered a sign of good luck and power as evidenced by this rhyme:

With a four-leaved Clover, a double-leaved
Ash, and green-topped Seave (rush),
You may go before the queen's daughter
without asking leave.

According to European custom, the ash tree had the power to keep away snakes and serpents. So strongly was this believed that women would hang their baby's cradle from an ash tree while they worked in the field, fully confident that the ash tree would protect the babies from crawling serpents.

Medicinally, ash was used by the American Indians as a strong laxative and as a tonic after childbirth. A tea made from the inner bark was used to treat stomach disorders and to promote sweating to break a fever. A solution made from this tree bark was used externally for sores, lice, and snakebites.

The seeds of the ash tree were considered an aphrodisiac.

Ash wood, which is strong with excellent shock resistance, is used most often in making sports equipment such as baseball bats, oars, and paddles. Other uses include making handles for shovels, spades, forks, hoes, and rakes. The wood also bends easily, making it good for the bent part of chairs. Used for church pews and bowling alleys, ash is welcomed everywhere that strength and lightness must be combined. The wood is dense (42 pounds per cubic foot). The heartwood is brown or dark brown.

COMMON NAME: *Aspen*

BOTANICAL NAME: *Populus tremuloides*

FAMILY: Salicaceae (Willow)

DESCRIPTION: Mature trees grow to a height of 40 to 50 feet. When young, the trees are narrow and straight, spreading as they grow older. The leaves are small, ovate to round, and flat-stalked. The thin bark is almost white at first; older specimens have bark that is black at the base. Flowers appear in early spring in catkins 1½ to 2½ inches long.

ORIGIN: Aspens grow throughout the northeastern, northern, and western parts of the United States, including Alaska.

HOW TO GROW: Aspens look best if used in groves and not as individual specimens. A grove of aspens looks particularly good in fall if planted against a backdrop of dark spruces and firs. Preferable growing conditions include full sun and rich, deep, well-drained soil. Aspens grow in zones 1 to 5.

Aspens are a wonderful testimony of the rejuvenating powers of nature. An aspen grove can reproduce and replace itself within fifty years. The trees are not long-lived, however, and begin to decay early in life just as they approach full growth. They have the greatest natural distribution of any tree in North America. Aspens grow everywhere in the United States except for the Atlantic coast south of New Jersey and the Ohio valley.

The name quaking aspen was given to this tree because the slightest breeze causes the leaves to tremble. The wind causes a soft, high, pleasant, delicate sound, and the upper surfaces of the leaves catch the light, making them almost twinkle.

There is a common belief that aspen was the wood from which the cross on which Jesus was crucified was formed and that the leaves tremble to this day in remembrance of this event. The Syrian name is *khashafa*, which means "to be agitated."

The Doctrine of Signatures, proposed by a seventeenth century Swiss physician, suggested that plants physically resemble the body parts they were destined to cure. Quaking aspen was frequently used to cure the ague, or diseases characterized by constant shaking.

Tea made from the root bark was used by American Indian women to ease menstrual cramps and stop excessive bleeding. A poultice made from the roots was used on cuts and bruises, and the tea, taken internally, was used to treat urinary disorders and diarrhea.

The bark contains salicin, an aspirinlike substance proven effective as an anti-inflammatory and an analgesic. The inner bark of aspen is quite bitter but is still sought after and eaten by beavers, who also use the trunks in building their dams. Snowshoe rabbits eat the bark and twigs, grouse eat the winter buds, and moose browse on the leaves throughout the year.

The wood is very light—only 25 pounds per cubic foot. It is soft, weak, and brittle. Aspen wood shrinks very little and bends quite well, particularly for a hardwood, but it does have a tendency to split under nails and screws. It will not take stain easily but can be painted. The cheese industry has long used aspen for containers because it is lightweight, light in color, and does not affect the odor or taste of the cheese. Today the wood is used to manufacture paper for magazines.

Aspens provide an important link in the evolution of the forest, as they are one of the first trees to repopulate areas that have been cut or burned. The seedlings grow and provide shade, which essentially acts as a "nursery" for hardwood seedlings that follow them.

A related species, Balsam poplar, is the state tree of Wyoming.

COMMON NAME: *Aucuba*

BOTANICAL NAME: *Aucuba japonica*

FAMILY: Cornaceae (Dogwood)

DESCRIPTION: An attractive shrub growing 6 to 8 feet tall, aucuba has dark green leaves specked with gold or yellow. The leaves are long and serrated; the blossoms, which appear in spring, are tiny purple flowers borne in panicles.

ORIGIN: Himalayas (south Asia) to Japan

HOW TO GROW: Because aucuba is tolerant of salt spray, it is commonly included in seaside gardens. The shrub is also tolerant of smog and urban conditions and is therefore often found in city gardens as well. The shrub can be grown in either sun or shade, although direct hot sun sometimes burns the leaf edges. It requires a good deal of water, being somewhat intolerant of drought conditions. To get the greatest number of berries, plant at least four female plants to every male plant. Although the plants can be grown from ripe seeds or from cuttings, it is most often grown from container-grown plants. Grows in zones 7 to 10.

Aucubas are considered the most common evergreen of English city and suburban gardens. These hardy shrubs survive grime, smog, neglect, salt air, and ill treatment. For this reason they are often shunned by discerning and discriminating gardeners in England. Because they are less common in American gardens, they are more appreciated in the United States.

The plants are considered easy to grow, though they need ample moisture spring through fall. They respond well to pruning, but it is not a necessity.

COMMON NAME: *Azalea*

BOTANICAL NAME: *Rhododendron* sp.

FAMILY: Ericaceae (Heath)

DESCRIPTION: Azaleas are in the *Rhodo-dendron* genus, and while all azaleas are rhodo-dendrons, not all commonly called rhododen-drons are azaleas. In general azaleas have small, narrow, pointed leaves that are somewhat hairy along the midrib. The blossoms of azaleas are found at the sides and tips of the flowering branch. Azalea flowers are either single, double, or "hose-in-hose," meaning that one single flower is set inside another single flower. The funnel-shaped flowers usually have five to ten stamens. As opposed to rhododendrons, which grow upright, many azalea species sprawl and grow in a spreading form. Azaleas can be divided into two main groups, native species and hybrids, which are the result of crossing two or more native species. North American native azaleas generally are deciduous, the hybrid species, evergreen.

Some of the most popular native azalea species include *R. kaempferi*, torch azalea, which has white, pink, orange, red, or salmon blos-soms measuring 2 inches across; *R. macrosepa-lum*, which has large pink or white flowers with large sepals; and *R. serpyllifolium*, wild thyme azalea, which grows only 4 feet tall and has small (½-inch) light pink blossoms.

Hybrid azalea groups include Beltsville hybrids, which grow 12 to 18 inches tall and have double and hose-in-hose flowers; Glenn Dale hybrids, which have large blooms that may appear from early to late spring; Girard hybrids, which are low growing and bloom in mid-spring; Greenwood hybrids (developed specifically for cool areas), which bloom early to mid-spring; and Pericat hybrids, which grow 2 to 6 feet tall with 2- to 2½-inch flowers.

ORIGIN: Azaleas are indigenous to most parts of the temperate northern hemisphere. Many azalea species are native to the United States (generally deciduous species), but the greatest concentration of native azalea species is in the Himalayas, southeastern Asia, and the mountains of Malaysia.

HOW TO GROW: In general azaleas prefer dappled sun or shady conditions. If the soil is kept constantly moist and the sun is not too intense, the plants can be grown in full sun. Azaleas like very rich soil, full of organic matter. They prefer slightly acidic soils that are well drained. Because the roots are shallow, the plants should be mulched. Cultivating around the base of the shrubs is discouraged because the roots can be easily damaged. Both azaleas and rhododendrons should be fed lightly in early spring. After flowering the shrubs benefit from judicious pruning.

The genus name *Rhododendron* means "rose tree" and refers to the beautiful blossoms occurring on almost all species in this genus. The name azalea is from the Greek word for "dry" and refers to the dry-woods habitat where this shrub is commonly found in the wild.

There are many species of azaleas native to the United States, particularly in the southeastern and northwestern parts of the country. Cultivated azaleas, which are primarily evergreen, were introduced into England from China in 1808 when the English East India Company established a factory in Canton. By 1810 *Azalea indica* was cultivated in Kew Gardens.

According to the English language of flowers, azalea is symbolic of temperance.

COMMON NAME: *Baldcypress*

BOTANICAL NAME: *Taxodium distichum*

FAMILY: Taxodiaceae (Baldcypress)

DESCRIPTION: This deciduous tree grows to be 100 feet tall and has a distinctly tapered trunk. In swampy or wet areas, the tree produces "knees," projections from the roots. The needlelike leaves are light green, creating a graceful, ferny look. Before the leaves drop in fall, they turn a bronze color. The bark is reddish brown.

ORIGIN: Delaware to Florida, west to Arkansas and Louisiana

HOW TO GROW: Baldcypress is surprisingly adaptable. Although in nature it is almost always found in swamps or extremely wet areas, it can be grown successfully in drier areas as well. The trees must have acid soil and full sun or partial shade. Baldcypress grows in zones 5 to 10.

Other than the American chestnut, baldcypress, unhappily, has had the greatest reduction of population of any other native tree. Baldcypress was once used extensively for shingles and posts and was much appreciated for its resistance to rot and insect damage. Most of the cypress used as lumber today is actually pondcypress, *Taxodium ascendens,* and not true baldcypress.

Although it is a conifer, baldcypress is deciduous and drops its leaves every autumn. This is where the name "bald" originated. Baldcypress is not a true cypress, but a member of the same family as the redwoods and sequoias.

Baldcypress grows most often in mucky swamps, but conditions here are difficult, even for this tree. The seeds can only germinate in soil that is saturated with water, but not flooded. This condition occurs sporadically in the swamp, and not always when seeds are available.

The seeds that are able to navigate the miracle of germination and grow to be the graceful, mystical baldcypress are few but are cherished

by tree lovers everywhere. The knees, which form the unusual bottom growth of these trees, arise from the shallow, widespread root system, but as yet, no cause or reason has been discovered for these lovely and strange protrusions.

Because it is resistant to decay, baldcypress is in demand for items such as boats and greenhouses. Care must be used when working with baldcypress, however, because the wood is very lightweight and tends to shrink while drying.

COMMON NAME: *Bamboo*

BOTANICAL NAME: *Phyllostachys nigra*

FAMILY: Gramineae (Grass)

DESCRIPTION: Although there is tremendous variation among bamboo species, in general bamboo grows to tree height. It has hollow, woody stems, with well-marked nodes. Several different genera are clumped together as "bamboo." These include *Phyllostachys nigra*, with leaves 5 inches long, toothed on the edges, and blue-green underneath (the stems turn black as they get older); *Arundinaria variegata*, with white striping on green leaves; *Bambusa multiples*, which has reddish green leaves with silvery undersides and forms clumps; and *Phyllostachys aurea*, with rigid yellow stems with narrow leaves about 5 inches long.

ORIGIN: Bamboo grows naturally throughout the tropical zone into the subtropics and sometimes into the temperate zone. Tropical Asia has a great wealth of bamboo populations. Three species are native to the United States.

HOW TO GROW: The problem with growing most bamboo is not in learning how to grow it but in learning how to contain it. Most bamboo species prefer full sun and moist conditions, an environment that often produces a population of bamboo difficult to control. Plant sparsely and weed diligently to keep them in check.

In Oriental countries bamboo is called "one of nature's most valuable gifts to uncivilized man" owing to the numerous uses of the wood. The possibilities of bamboo uses are endless. Bamboo wood holds a unique combination of qualities. The wood is light, hollow, flexible, and strong. Among a thousand other things, the wood is used for fencing and furniture; for water buckets and bottles; as timber for building houses, for flooring, and for making rafters; as masts for

ships; for making baskets, umbrellas, and walking sticks.

There are more than 1,000 species of bamboo in the *Bambuseae* genus. Botanically, bamboo is considered a grass.

Bamboos exhibit what is known as synchrony, the phenomenon of simultaneous growth: Genetically related plants set seed, germinate, grow, and then flower all at the same time. In the case of bamboo, millions of acres

may burst into bloom at the same time, having not bloomed for decades. Records tell us that bamboo forests in China flowered in 919 B.C., and in 115 B.C.; after being transplanted in Japan, they flowered again in 1730 and 1845. The latest record of bamboo flowering in synchrony is in England and Alabama where, in both locations, flowering occured in the 1960s.

In China bamboo is much revered because large clumps stand up to hurricanes better than almost any other kind of tree. An Englishman wrote in the 1860s: "What would a poor Chinaman do without the bamboo? Independently of its use as a food, it provides him with the thatch that covers his house, the mat on which he sleeps, the cup from which he drinks, and the chopsticks with which he eats."

Bamboo played a crucial part in a modern invention. Thomas Edison used a carbonized filament from bamboo for making his early incandescent light bulbs. This bamboo filament was used in the manufacturing of light bulbs until 1910, when it was replaced by thin metal wires.

Bamboo is the major food source for giant pandas who feed on the leaves, shoots, and stalks of dwarf species of bamboo in the *Dendrocalamus* genera. It is also the major food source for the mountain gorillas of Zaire. Young bamboo shoots of the genus *Phyllostachys* are edible and are important economically as a food source in central China.

Bamboo has played an important role in Oriental history since the time of the Chinese Tang dynasty.

COMMON NAME: *Barberry*
BOTANICAL NAME: *Berberis wilsoniae*
FAMILY: Berberidaceae (Barberry)

DESCRIPTION: This species of barberry is semievergreen and grows 3 feet tall, spreading to a width of 6 feet. The dull green leaves measure 1 inch long. The mature stems are dark red and grooved. In general barberries are rounded, thorny shrubs with small yellow flowers. They make a good hedge or foundation plant, particularly when a barrier is needed.

ORIGIN: Most species of this genus are native to South America and eastern Asia.

HOW TO GROW: Barberries need moist, well-drained soil. They are easy to propagate by separating the seeds from the pulp and sowing in autumn. They like sun or partial shade and should be pruned lightly to help give the plant a nice shape. Although small container-grown plants do well when moved, larger, more-established bushes do not transplant well. Barberry grows in zones 6 to 8.

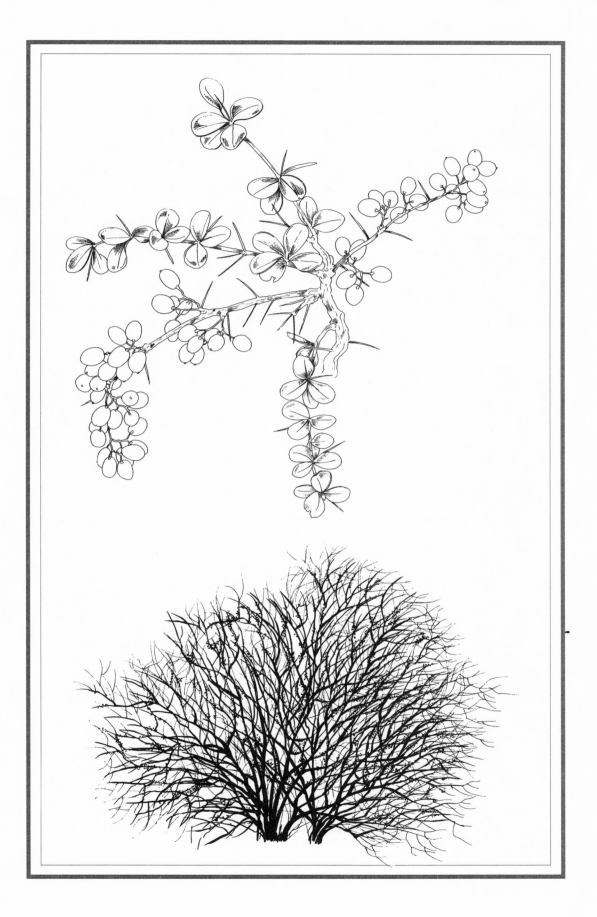

According to the Doctrine of Signatures of a seventeenth-century Swiss physician, the yellow wood of common barberry, *B. vulgaris,* was used to treat jaundice. Although of questionable importance as treatment for jaundice, the chemicals within the bark and roots of this plant made it effective in relieving diarrhea.

Berberine, a substance extracted from the plant, is even today used in eye medicines. Ancient Egyptians treated disease with the bark mixed with fennel seeds. The antibacterial quali-ties of the plant probably made it an effective folk medicine in many cultures. Tea made from the root bark served as an astringent and an antiseptic. Tea made from the leaves was useful in treating coughs, and a tincture from the root bark was used for treating arthritis and rheumatism. Large doses of this are considered harmful.

The wood is used successfully in marquetry work, as the light yellow color contasts beautifully with darker wood.

COMMON NAME: *Beech, American*
BOTANICAL NAME: *Fagus grandifolia*
FAMILY: Fagaceae (Beech)

DESCRIPTION: In full growth the American beech reaches a height of 80 to 100 feet and is characterized by its smooth light gray bark. The coarsely toothed leaves are oblong (4 to 7 inches long) and oval. They are blue-green on top and light green underneath and turn a lovely golden yellow in fall. Leaves often persist on the tree throughout winter. Surface roots are often conspicuous. European beech, *F. sylvatica,* is widely cultivated as a shade tree. It grows to 70 feet or more and has a trunk diameter of 2½ feet. The leaves have edges with small teeth and are shiny dark green on top. In autumn these leaves turn reddish brown or bronze. This species is grown often in the northeastern United States and in the Pacific states. It likes cool, moist temperatures.

ORIGIN: American beech is native to the eastern part of North America, north of Florida.

HOW TO GROW: Beeches need full sun and rich, well-drained soil. They are large, stately trees and are good specimen plants, providing deep shade.

The genus (and family) name *Fagus* is from the Greek word meaning "to eat," which refers to the edible nuts. The words *beech* and *book* are from the same root, referring to the ancient Saxon and Germanic practice of carving runic characters on boards from beech trees.

Beech wood is heavy, averaging 45 pounds per cubic foot. It is very strong and shock resistant and can be bent if properly steamed. In appearance beech wood has tiny pores and outstanding rays. While seasoning, beech has a high propensity for shrinking. Beech wood is used as lumber and as veneer. It has often been used in the food industry because it does not release flavor or odor. The wood is used to make flooring, crates, and tool handles.

Beech bark was used for tanning, and the ashes from burned wood were used for potash. Beech leaves were used to stuff mattresses; the fragrance from the leaves was thought to keep away bugs. Oil extracted from the seeds was said to be "little inferior to olive oil, and fit for burning." The oil from the nuts was also sometimes used in cooking. The pulp from the seeds was thought to be sweeter than wheat flour. Particularly in the southern United States, the leaves were used as a potherb, and the nuts were ground as a substitute for coffee.

However sweet they are thought to be, beech seeds sometimes present a certain danger. Some reports have been made of people experiencing vertigo after eating them. Presumably the ill effects were caused from fagine, a slightly narcotic chemical found in beechnut husks. Large amounts of beech bark and leaves may be poisonous to both people and animals.

Rappahannock Indians used the bark steeped in saltwater to make a salve to soothe burns, frostbite, and the rash from poison ivy (the ratio was one ounce bark to one pint of salt water).

A Kentucky recipe used sap from the tree to make a syrup to treat tuberculosis. Leaves and bark were made into an ointment to soothe burns, sores, and ulcers. Internally it was used to treat problems of the bladder, kidney, and liver.

An outstanding characteristic of the beech tree is its clear, soft bark, which has been irresistible to graffiti writers for many centuries. Even in Roman times this tree was subject to vandalism, as was reported in the Latin proverb *"Crescent illae; crescetis amores,"* meaning "as these letters grow, so may our love," which refers to the initials of lovers carved into the bark of the beech tree.

According to superstition beech trees planted near the house were thought to keep away lightning. This may be of more value than many other legendary "lightning trees," as records indicate that beech trees are struck by lightning less often than any other kind of tree, possibly because of the high oil content of the trunk.

COMMON NAME: *Birch, River*
BOTANICAL NAME: *Betula nigra*
FAMILY: Betulaceae (Birch)

DESCRIPTION: There are approximately fifty to sixty different species of birches, most of which are native to North America and Asia. The trees (or sometimes shrubs) generally grow to a height of 40 to 100 feet. The alternate leaves are toothed, with straight veins. The tree, which has slender branches, also bears flowers in early spring. Birch bark varies in color from one species to another from white to silver, yellowish, to reddish brown and almost black.

ORIGIN: Most birches are native to North America and Asia.

HOW TO GROW: Birches look good in a wood border. In general they prefer cool, moist soils and full sunlight and do not like to be transplanted. The best time to plant balled (bound roots in a large burlap ball) or container-grown young trees is in early spring. Birches do not do well in drought conditions and are often subject to various pests during a dry spell.

Perhaps the most famous reference to birch bark is in Henry Wadsworth Longfellow's poem "The Song of Hiawatha":

Give me of your bark, O Birch-tree!
Of your yellow bark, O birch tree!
I a light canoe will build me
That shall float upon the river.

The idea of a birch-bark canoe has been firmly planted in our imaginations for many years, based on this popular poem. The American Indians did indeed take the bark from the birch tree to make canoes; they also used the bark for making wigwams and various utensils. It took many different kinds of trees to produce a finished canoe. The frames for birch-bark canoes were made from northern white cedar. They were covered with birch bark and sewn together with thread made from tamarack roots; the seams were caulked with pine or balsam-fir resin.

Paper birch wood is easily worked. The white wood is used for making small items such as bas-

kets, toy canoes, dowels, ice-cream sticks, and toothpicks. The bark is easily removed from the tree, and unless the entire tree is debarked, removal does not injure the tree. It does, however, leave ugly black scars, and this practice is definitely discouraged. Because birch wood polishes beautifully, it is often used for flooring. Its resiliency makes it particularly good for flooring on basketball courts. When freshly cut, birch wood has a rosy tint, which deepens in color as it ages.

Sap from the tree was sometimes used in medicines. Alcohol was extracted from the sap by a process of evaporation and fermentation. The wintergreen fragrance from the bark and leaves was probably used extensively for flavoring medicines.

B. lenta has many common names including cherry birch, black birch, mahogany birch, and mountain mahogany. This species grows particularly well in the Appalachian mountains. During the nineteenth century there was a great demand for the clean, minty oil extracted from the birch tree. Mountaineers nearly caused the extinction

of this tree, chopping it down to sell the oil made from the bark and twigs. Luckily scientists learned to make the same flavoring synthetically, thus saving the trees.

Tea made from the twigs and bark was used as a remedy for rheumatism in southern Appalachia. Birch-bark oil, which has astringent properties, was used externally to soothe sprains and cuts. Today the oil is used quite effectively to relieve sore and strained muscles.

In Scandinavia birch was considered sacred to the god Thor. Country folks would hang birch branches indoors as tribute to Thor, who would in turn supposedly protect the home from various afflictions such as lightning, the "evil eye," and infertility.

According to the Victorian language of flowers, however, the birch is a symbol of grace and meekness. The American Forestry Association chose the birch as their first Mother Tree of America in 1920.

White birch is the state tree of New Hampshire.

COMMON NAME: *Boxelder*

BOTANICAL NAME: *Acer negundo*

FAMILY: Aceraceae (Maple)

DESCRIPTION: The small boxelder tree grows to a height of 30 to 60 feet. The light gray bark has narrow furrows and deep ridges. It usually branches several times at irregular intervals and has a broad crown. The flowers come in spring, male and female occurring on separate trees. Blossoms are clustered together on slender flowering stalks. The leaves are pinnately compound, having three to seven leaflets, and are pointed on the ends.

ORIGIN: Boxelder is native from central Canada south to Texas, east to Florida, and north to southern New England.

HOW TO GROW: Boxelder is in the same genus as maples and has similar cultural requirements. Grow in partial shade or full sun in moist, well-drained soil. In nature boxelder grows along stream banks and in moist soils. It is hardy to zone 3.

Boxelder is very similar to the maple tree except that it has pinnately compound leaves. Very fast growing, it is often used for shade or shelter, but because it is easily broken in storms, it is sometimes deemed unsatisfactory as a garden plant.

Boxelder was extensively planted for a quick spot of shade, particularly in the Midwest. Although the tree does grow quickly, it is some-

what short-lived. Boxelder attains a greater size in cultivation than it does in the wild. The largest one on record is found in White Plains, New York. It reaches a height of 75 feet and has a spread of 102 feet.

Other than its speedy growth, boxelder seems to have few qualities to recommend its inclusion in the garden. The wood is soft, brittle,

and weak, weighing only 27 pounds per cubic foot. The sapwood and heartwood look very similar, and both are light in color. The wood is essentially useless except to burn as fuel. The leaves do not turn colors in the fall but simply turn brown and drop. The Kansas State Board of Agriculture thought so little of the boxelder that its bulletin on trees included this statement: "There is no excuse for planting this tree."

In the West, however, where boxelder is one of the few shade trees capable of tolerating the harsh conditions found there, it receives more acclaim. In the West, too, boxelder leaves seem to turn prettier colors and often show hues of yellow and red in autumn.

Boxelder also yields a sweet sap from which syrup can be made, similar to that made from maple sugar. The sap of boxelder is not nearly as sweet as that of the maples but was of sufficient worth to be used by all the Native American tribes of the Missouri River basin.

The only known medicinal use of boxelder was a tea made from the inner bark sometimes used to induce vomiting. American Indians also used the wood to make charcoal for ceremonial painting and tattooing.

COMMON NAME: *Buckeye, Ohio*

BOTANICAL NAME: *Aesculus glabra*

FAMILY: Hippocastanaceae (Horsechestnut)

DESCRIPTION: Buckeye usually grows to about 35 feet but sometimes reaches a height of up to 60 feet. It is a dense tree, and the leaves come out very early in spring. The leaves are 3 to 6 inches long, elliptic in shape. The blossoms are pale yellow and occur in panicles in mid-spring. The egg-shaped fruit is 1 to 2½ inches long. *A. glabra* is native from West Virginia and western Pennsylvania south to Alabama and Tennessee. California buckeye, *A. californica,* is a small tree that grows about 25 feet tall. The leaves are palmately compound and are divided into five leaflets.

ORIGIN: California buckeye is found in California coastal ranges and on western slopes up to about 5,000 feet.

HOW TO GROW: Ohio Buckeye needs moist but not wet conditions, full sun, and slightly acidic soil. If grown in good conditions, fall foliage is yellow or orange. It makes a good ornamental tree but has the disadvantage of litter from leaves, flowers, and fruit. Grows in zones 5 to 8.

The name buckeye is thought to have been given to this tree because the shiny brown nuts look like the big brown eyes found on deer. Because the sap of *A. glabra* smells so bad, it was some- times known as fetid, or stinking buckeye.

California buckeye is the only western native species. Although the seeds are poisonous, the Indians would leach out the toxins with boiling

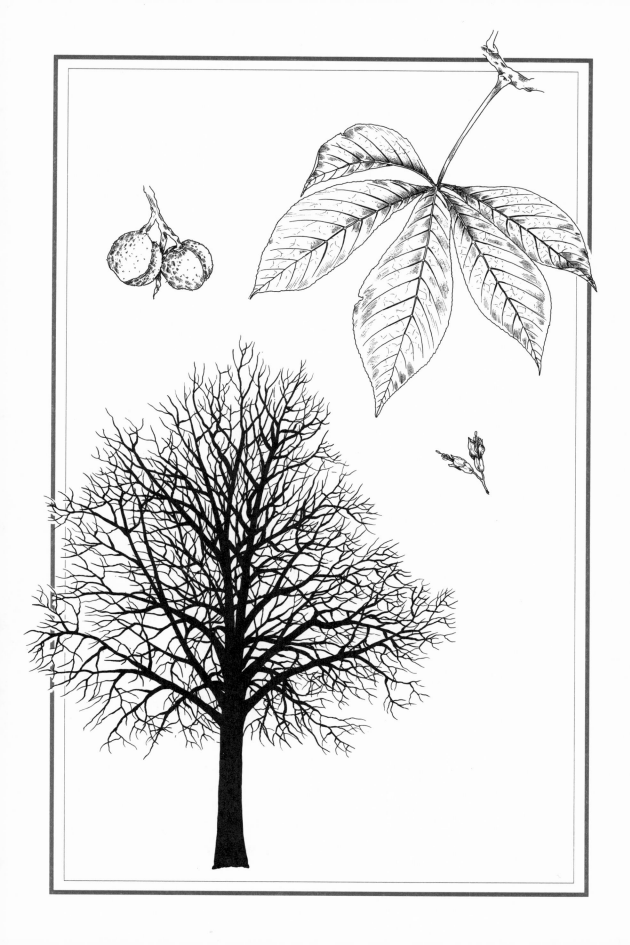

water and then grind the seeds into meal. The poisonous seeds were sometimes left untreated and thrown into a fish pond to temporarily stupefy the fish. The fish would then float to the surface, where they were easily caught.

The nuts were sometimes made into an ointment applied externally for rheumatism and piles. Although they are considered toxic, the nuts were sometimes taken internally in very, very small doses to ease cough spasms or asthma.

Ohio buckeye has soft, nearly white wood

that is used for manufacturing paper and for making luggage and toys. Before synthetic materials became widely used, buckeye was often used to make artificial limbs.

The wood of California buckeye is close-grained, soft, and light, weighing 31 pounds per cubic foot. The wood is white, with a slight reddish hue.

Buckeye is the state tree of Ohio, known as the Buckeye State.

COMMON NAME: *Burningbush*

BOTANICAL NAME: *Euonymus atropurpureus*

FAMILY: Celastraceae (Staff-Tree)

DESCRIPTION: The outstanding feature of this shrub is the beautifully colored seed capsules. Bright red or purple four-lobed and four-celled fruits often hang on slender stems throughout winter. The flowers are ⅛ inch wide and have dark purple or red petals. The height of the shrub is generally 20 feet or less; the leaves are opposite and pointed at the tip.

ORIGIN: Burningbush is native from New York south to Georgia and west to Texas and North Dakota.

HOW TO GROW: Euonymus prefers moist soils and does best when planted at the edge of a wood where it receives partial sun.

Euonymus, also knowns as eastern wahoo, is most conspicuous when the brightly colored seeds have ripened. *Atropurpureus,* the species name, is from Latin and means "dark purple," referring to the color of the fruit. The name *Euonymus* was given to this genus by Linnaeus. The name means "of auspicious name" and refers to the supposed great medicinal value found in many of the species.

The bark of euonymus was ground into a

powder and used by American Indians and pioneers as a purgative. Another species of euonymus, *E. europaeus* is commonly known as the European spindletree and has bright red autumn leaves and large showy red berries. At one time concoctions were made from the bark of this tree and were used extensively by early physicians and folk healers as a purge and a strong laxative. This medicine proved to be so strong, however, that drastic purging and inter-

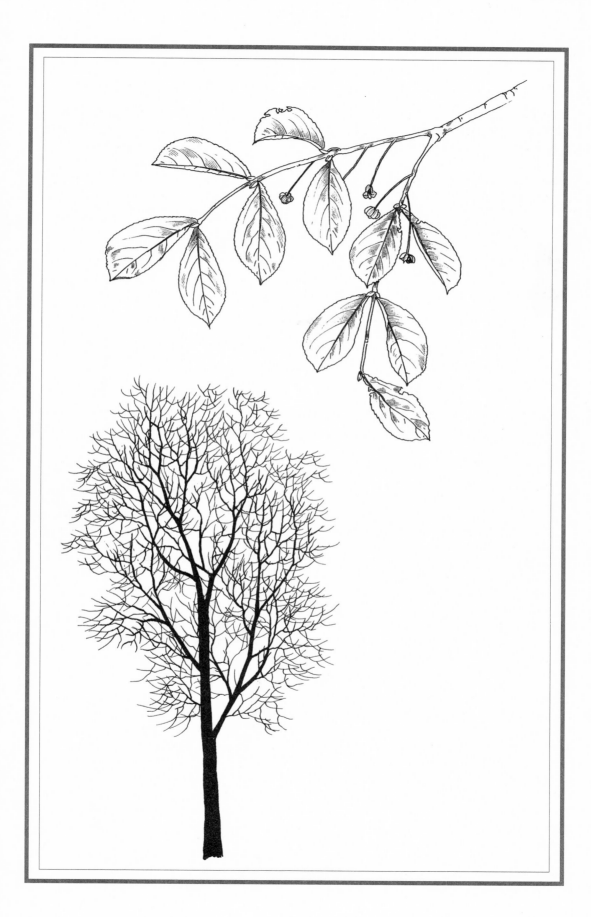

nal damage often resulted, causing the U.S. Food and Drug Administration to declare it unsafe for medical purposes.

The bark of *E. atropurpureus* was given as a general tonic, a laxative and expectorant. Syrup made from the bark was used to treat fever and upset stomach. Both the bark and the root con-

tain compounds similar to those found in foxglove.

The wood is often much sought after by sculptors, and artists prefer charcoal made from this tree. The bark was considered superior to all others for tanning fine leather.

COMMON NAME: *Camellia*

BOTANICAL NAME: *Camellia japonica*

FAMILY: Theaceae (Tea)

DESCRIPTION: Japanese camellia is a deciduous shrub growing 5 to 12 feet in height. The 3-inch-long oval leaves are thick and leathery. Camellia blossoms are spectacularly beautiful and come in shades of pink, red, and white. They measure 5 inches across, with five to six petals. There are thousands of named cultivars differing in flower colors, sizes, and forms.

ORIGIN: coastal regions of Japan, South Korea, and Taiwan

HOW TO GROW: These shrubs should be planted in acidic, rich, moist, well-drained soil. They put forth shallow roots, which are best mulched and then left alone. They need even moisture but little fertilizer and should be protected from winter sun. Because they bloom during winter and very early spring, they are often subject to cold damage. They should be pruned after blooming. Camellias grow in zones 8 to 10.

The camellia was named for a Moravian Jesuit priest, George J. Kamel. The spelling was changed to Camellus and given the feminine gender ending, camellia. Kamel went to Manila in 1682. Here he not only performed his missionary duties but also wrote a comprehensive book on the plants of the Philippines.

According to Chinese folklore, the courtyard of Yao had two kinds of trees growing there that were of great importance to the people. On one side of the garden stood a tree that put forth one

leaf every day for fifteen days as the moon waxed. Next to it stood a tree that shed one leaf every day for fifteen days as the moon waned. In this way the Chinese kept track of the months. On the other side of the garden stood a tree that put forth one leaf every month for six months. Next to it stood a tree that shed one leaf every month for six months. In this way they kept track of the years. Traditionally these trees were surrounded by beautiful camellia shrubs. The camellia is cherished in Japan as well. It is con-

sidered the flower for December in the Japanese Floral Calendar.

According to the English language of flowers, camellia means "perfected loveliness" or "unpretending excellence." In Germany this flower means "Thou art my heart's sovereign."

COMMON NAME: *Camphor-tree*

BOTANICAL NAME: *Cinnamomum camphora*

FAMILY: Lauraceae (Laurel)

DESCRIPTION: This rounded, dense evergreen tree grows to a height of 100 feet or more. The trunk diameter is about 2 feet. The pointed leaves are 2 to 4 inches long and have three main veins. The leaves are slightly pinkish when young, turning shiny green as they age. The gray bark develops rough, thickened furrows as it matures. Yellowish clusters of flowers appear in spring, followed by single-seeded black berries in fall.

ORIGIN: Camphor-tree is native to China, Taiwan, and Japan but is now grown extensively in Florida, southern Texas, and southern California.

HOW TO GROW: In nature camphor-tree is found in moist spots in humid subtropical areas. It is hardy to zone 9.

In the deep South, camphor-tree is often grown as a street tree because of its great and soothing shade.

In its native countries the bark and leaves are distilled to obtain camphor oil and gum, which is used in medicines and in industry. The leaves of camphor-tree are harvested three or four times a year, and the trees are pruned to a height of 5 to 6 feet for this purpose. Oil is extracted from the leaves and made into camphor crystals, which have extensive applications worldwide.

Camphor crystals have been credited with many powers, including the ability to cure the common cold. Often folk healers would suggest that their patients wear a small bag of camphor crystals around their neck for this reason. This practice is no longer recommended, however, as modern testing has discovered that extended exposure to the crystals can cause poisoning. Today the crystals are used medicinally only in the creation of lotions and salves useful in relieving external itches and pain. Camphor crystals are also used industrially to make deodorants, disinfectants, explosives, insecticides, perfumes, and soap.

The active ingredient in the wood of camphor-tree is a chemical, 2-bornanone, commonly known as camphor, a strong moth repellent. The wood was used extensively to make chests for sailors because it was resistant to decay from salt air and impervious to damage from most

kinds of insects. The wood is useful in repelling insects as well and is still used for making chests of drawers and cabinets.

A closely related species, *C. zeylanicum,* is the source for commercial cinnamon. The bark is stripped from shoots of the tree, dried in the sun, and then ground into a fine powder. Although the bark from *C. cassia* is also used for this purpose, the fragrance and flavor are not as delicate or good and is therefore not as desirable.

COMMON NAME: *Catalpa, Southern*

BOTANICAL NAME: *Catalpa bignonioides*

FAMILY: Bignoniaceae (Trumpet Creeper)

DESCRIPTION: This genus has large, long-stalked leaves and showy, two-lipped flowers. The fruit is a long cylinder. *C. bignonioides* has broad oval leaves that emit an unpleasant odor when crushed. The flowers appear in spring and are large and long with yellow-striped insides and purple-brown spots. The tree grows to be 30 to 40 feet tall and has a short trunk and rounded top. In fall the fruit forms in pods, which are 9 to 14 inches long. Northern catalpa, *C. speciosa,* grows to be about 60 feet tall and has a dark reddish brown trunk. The blooms on this species appear earlier in spring than do those on the southern catalpa. Northern catalpa grows from southwestern Indiana to northeastern Arkansas and is often cultivated in the West.

ORIGIN: Southern catalpa is native to southeastern United States but is now naturalized in the northeast as well.

HOW TO GROW: Catalpas are very fast-growing, short-lived trees. They can be grown in ordinary garden soil and tolerate both wet and dry conditions. Grows in zones 5 to 9.

Both northern and southern species of Catalpa are called cigartree and Indian-bean, referring to the interesting fruit formed on the trees.

Tea made from the bark was used externally as an antiseptic and to treat snakebites. Tea made from the seeds was used for pulmonary disorders. The tea was also sometimes used as a sedative. A poultice made from the leaves was put on wounds and cuts. The pods were thought to be effective as a sedative. Today they are thought to hold cardioactive properties.

Catalpas are among the oldest cultivated trees in China. The Chinese species *C. ovata* and *C. bungei* were planted for their high-quality, easily worked timber. The flowers of both these species are slightly larger than those of their American cousins.

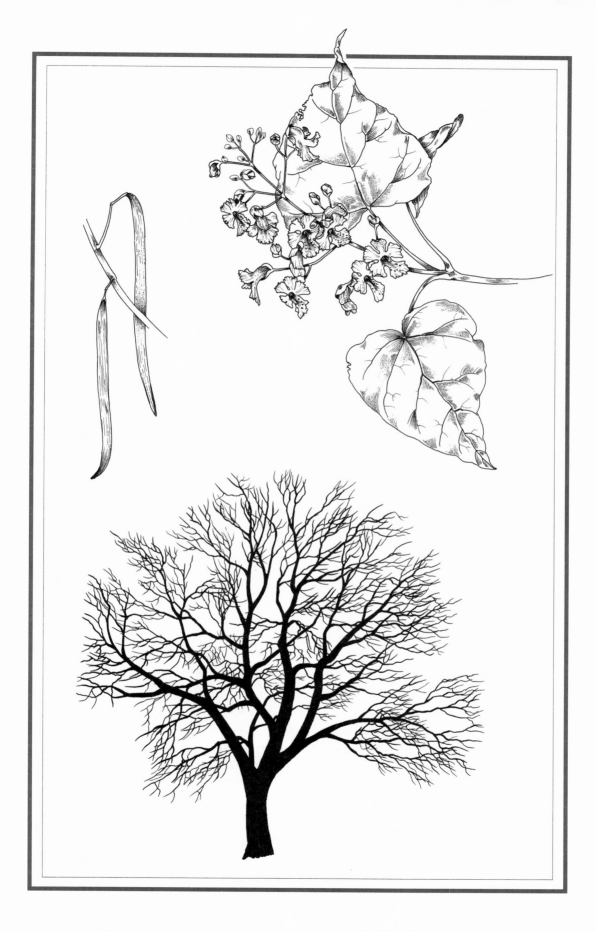

COMMON NAME: *Cedar-of-Lebanon*

BOTANICAL BAME: *Cedrus libani*

FAMILY: Pinaceae (Pine)

DESCRIPTION: Cedars are characterized by stiff, needlelike evergreen leaves. Cedar-of-Lebanon is about 100 feet tall at maturity and generally has either a single trunk or several large trunklike branches. The brown cones, which can be found on the tree throughout the year, are 3 to 4 inches long. *C. atlantica,* blue atlas cedar, grows 40 to 60 feet tall and has silvery blue needles. This tree spreads to about ¾ of its height.

ORIGIN: Asia Minor and Syria

HOW TO GROW: Cedars like ordinary garden soil and open areas. They do not transplant well and do best when planted as container-grown plants. Young trees should be watered well and should not be allowed to dry out. Cedars grow in zones 5 to 8.

Cedar-of-Lebanon has a massive trunk and a flat-topped crown. The barrel-shaped cones take two years to mature. After they mature, the cones disintegrate on the tree. In its native lands harvesting of cedar-of-Lebanon is illegal. In the United States its timber is used in the construction business, for paneling, and for making furniture.

The growth of Atlantic white cedar, or blue atlas cedar, is often hampered by greenbriar, a thorny vine that winds its way up the tree and then grows profusely at treetop level where it has access to the sun. The weight of the vine often breaks the trunks of the trees.

Wildlife, too, deters great growth of these trees. White-tailed deer eat the young sprouts, and meadow mice girdle very young trees.

The trees are quite resistant to damage by fungi and insects, however, as they contain chemicals that act as natural fungicides and thus make the wood particularly durable.

Northern white cedar is not a true cedar but is known botanically as *Thjua occidentalis.* It is called cedar because the scent of the oil from the tree is very similar to that of true cedar. A sixteenth-century king of France called it *l'arbre de vie,* or "the tree of life." It was not the beauty of the tree that earned it this esteemed name but the medicine extracted from it.

Explorers on the St. Lawrence River died of scurvy in great numbers before the Native Americans showed them how to boil branches and foliage of the northern white cedar to create a concoction that was rich enough in vitamins to combat scurvy. Europeans were so impressed with this cure that they introduced white cedar into medicinal gardens of Europe. Some say that this was the first tree species from America to be introduced to Europe. Even today a medicinal concoction used to treat colds is derived from cedar.

White cedar has very light wood and is so bouyant that fishermen sometimes make decoy minnows from it. The durable wood is used by railroadmen to make crossties. It is also used to make canoe ribs, as it separates easily into thin,

flexible slats. This characteristic also makes it important for making pails, boats, and even water tanks.

A related species of northern white cedar is western red cedar, *T. plicata*, which has a highly aromatic wood. It is also known as canoe cedar,

Idaho cedar, shinglewood, and stinking cedar. It grows from southern Alaska to northern California, east to Montana and Idaho. As the common names indicate, wood from this tree is generally used to make boats and shingles.

COMMON NAME: *Cherokee Rose*

BOTANICAL NAME: *Rosa laevigata*

FAMILY: Rosaceae (Rose)

DESCRIPTION: Cherokee rose is a tall shrub that sometimes grows as high as 15 feet. The leaves are shiny green, and the flowers are large (3½ inches long), white, and fragrant. The entire plant is covered with small thorns or prickles. It blooms May through June.

ORIGIN: China, naturalized in upland regions of Georgia, Alabama, Tennessee, and North and South Carolina

HOW TO GROW: Because this plant has a rather ragged growth form, it is rarely cultivated. It is quite attractive, however, when in full bloom and for this reason is sometimes included within a garden or a planted woodland area. For best results plant it in an area that receives partial shade and supply it with even moisture until the plant becomes established.

Cherokee rose is not native to the United States but was imported by way of England in the middle of the eighteenth century.

A lovely legend about the Cherokee rose is popular in the South, where the shrub grows. A young Cherokee Indian girl lived with her family in the mountains of North Carolina. Her tribe frequently fought with neighboring tribes, and, during one of these skirmishes, a young man from an enemy tribe was wounded and captured.

When this man was brought into the camp,

the young girl asked her father, chief of the tribe, if she could nurse the prisoner back to health. Reluctantly her father gave his permission, and for days and nights the young woman sat by his bedside, coaxing the wounded man to eat and dressing his wounds.

Inevitably the young man and the young woman fell in love, and the captured man begged the girl to run away and return with him to his home. Although the girl loved him, she hesitated a long time before answering because

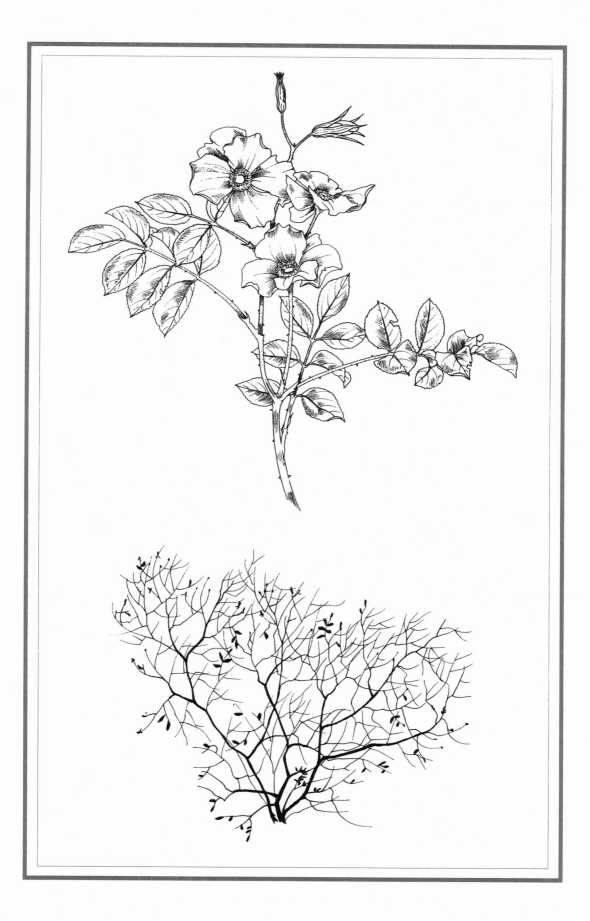

she knew that if she left her home with the handsome brave, she would never be able to return.

But love won out in the end. Before dawn one morning, the young brave and the girl slipped out of camp and headed toward the north country. Before she left, though, the girl bent and plucked a piece of the rose growing beside her father's home. She took it with her to plant in her new home to remind herself of the village that she had left behind. This rose is now called the Cherokee rose.

Cherokee rose is the state flower of Georgia.

COMMON NAME: *Cherry*
BOTANICAL NAME: *Prunus* sp.
FAMILY: Rosaceae (Rose)

DESCRIPTION: The genus *Prunus* comprises 400 species and includes stone fruits such as plums, almonds, peaches, and cherries as well as many ornamental trees and shrubs. Many different kinds of cherries are used in the landscape, the more ornamental of which have inedible fruit. The leaves are alternate and entire, never compound. The trees typically grow 30 to 50 feet tall. Blossoms are white, pink, or red, usually with five petals and five sepals. *P. sargentii*, Sargent cherry, is one of the best ornamental cherries. It grows 40 to 50 feet tall, has reddish brown bark, and produces lovely pink flowers in early spring. The fruit is small and unimportant. Grows in zones 5 to 8. Origin: Japan. *P. cerasifera*, cherry plum, grows to be 25 feet tall and produces white flowers. The fruit is either red or yellow. Grows in zones 5 to 9. Origin: central Asia. *P. serotina*, black cherry, grows 50 to 60 feet tall and produces edible black fruits. Leaves turn yellow in fall. Grows in zones 4 to 9. Origin: eastern North America from Nova Scotia to Florida. *P. serrulata* 'Kwanzan', Oriental cherry, is vase-shaped and grows to a height of 30

feet. The flowers appear in spring and are double, having up to thirty petals each. Leaves turn bronze in fall. Grows in zones 5 to 8. Origin: Japan. *P. subhirtella* 'Pendula', weeping Higan cherry, is a gracefully drooping tree with slender branches. The light pink flowers occur in clusters of 2 to 5 in early spring. Grows in zones 6 to 8. Origin: Japan. *P. yedoensis*, Yoshino cherry, is quite beautiful and showy, growing 40 feet in height. The flowers are pink or white and occur in clusters. Many cultivars have been developed from this species. This is the tree planted so extensively in Washington, D.C. Grows in zones 6 to 8. Origin: Japan.

ORIGIN: See Description.

HOW TO GROW: Cherries need full sun or partial shade and very well-drained soil. They are, in general, relatively short-lived, lasting only about thirty years under normal conditions. Frequent watering, mulch, selective pruning, and prompt attention to pests and disease may extend their life span.

The inner bark of cherries is quite aromatic and was used for many years as an ingredient in cough syrups and tinctures. Concoctions made from cherry trees were used to treat sore throat, diarrhea, respiratory ailments, persistent cough, and poor circulation. The bark was used as an ingredient in general tonics and to expel worms. As a poultice, it was used externally on ulcers and abcesses.

Black cherry bark, leaves, and seeds, unlike those of other species of cherries, contain highly toxic substances, particularly when the fruit ripens in fall.

Wild cherries were listed in the *United States Pharmacopeia* from 1800 to 1975.

In addition to a multitude of cultivated varieties, there are also several native species of cherries, including western chokecherry, *P. virginiana*. Native from British Columbia south to San Diego County, California, it is also found eastward as far as Lake Michigan.

The fruit of chokecherry is quite bitter but was eaten extensively by American Indians. Sacajawea was eating chokecherries when she was captured by Minatarees and sold as a slave child to a French trader. Sacajawea was later discovered by Lewis and Clark, and she ultimately served as a guide for them in their explorations.

The Navajo Indians considered chokecherry a sacred plant and used the wood to make prayer sticks. The black fruits were considered representative of the North and were used extensively in rituals and chants.

The plant was so important to the Plains Indians that the time during which the tree was in fruit was called "black-cherry-moon." The fruit is so small that it is impossible to remove the pits, so the Plains Indians pounded the entire cherry and ground it into a paste, which was used to make small cakes.

The cherry tree is symbolic of education. A white cherry tree, however, means deception.

COMMON NAME: *Chestnut, American*

BOTANICAL NAME: *Castanea dentata*

FAMILY: Fagaceae (Beech)

DESCRIPTION: In its prime American chestnut was a very large tree, growing to 100 feet or more. The leaves are long and narrow, pointed at the ends. The bark is a dark brownish gray. The majority of the flowers are male and occur in upright catkins 6 to 8 inches long. The female flowers are found at the base of shorter catkins. (Today the American chestnut is most often found in the form of shoots growing from the base of dead trees. Sometimes older trees can be found in western states where the chestnut blight was not as severe. The blight first hit in New York City in 1904, and over the course of the next forty years virtually wiped out the chestnut population in the United States.) Chinese chestnut, *C. mollissima*, is often grown as a substitute for the American chestnut. It is shorter, growing to a height of only 40 to 60 feet, and has leaves that appear red when emerging.

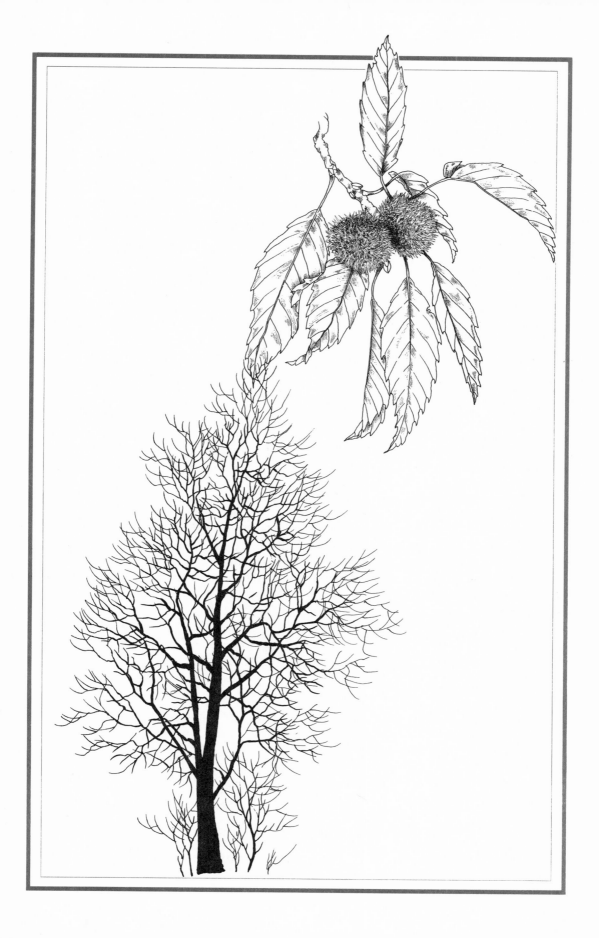

ORIGIN: American chestnut was native to much of eastern United States from Maine south to northern Florida.

HOW TO GROW: Chinese chestnut likes full sun, rich, sandy, acidic soil, and frequent fertilization. Although drought tolerant, young trees require plenty of water to become established. Grows in zones 4 to 8.

The species name *dentata* means "toothed," which refers to the leaf edges.

Both the fruit and the bark of the American chestnut were valuable. The bark was a source of tannin used in the leather industry. Wood sold as "wormy chestnut" is actually wood that was eaten by small insects after the tree was killed by the blight.

Chestnut blight, which killed thousands of American chestnut trees, was thought to have been brought to the United States in 1904, presumably on a shipment of nursery stock. First discovered at The New York Botanical Garden, the disease was identified as a fungus. Soon the disease spread to neighboring states and killed forest chestnuts as well as those used in the landscape. Within forty years this disease virtually wiped out the American chestnut tree.

In spite of the horrendous blight, there is no danger of the tree becoming extinct. Shoots frequently appear from dead trees. Blight-resistant varieties have been developed by crossing American and Chinese chestnuts.

Pioneers had a myriad of uses for chestnut trees. The bark was used for roofing material, the lumber for building houses and making furniture. Because the boards did not warp or shrink while drying, they were particularly prized by woodworkers.

The nuts, of course, are tasty treats for us today. In years past they were a staple food for many southern European communities. The nuts are very high in vitamins B_1, B_2, and C and are rich in starch and oils. They are eaten roasted or boiled or are sometimes ground into a flour used as a thickening agent.

Astringent qualities of the leaves, twigs, and bark make them good to use in treating cuts or sores. Chestnut tea was sometimes used to treat the symptoms of whooping cough.

In addition to its many uses, the American chestnut was a very beautiful tree as well. Henry Wadsworth Longfellow, in his poem "The Village Blacksmith," wrote of the "spreading chestnut tree."

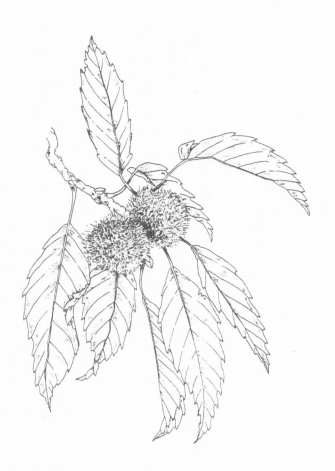

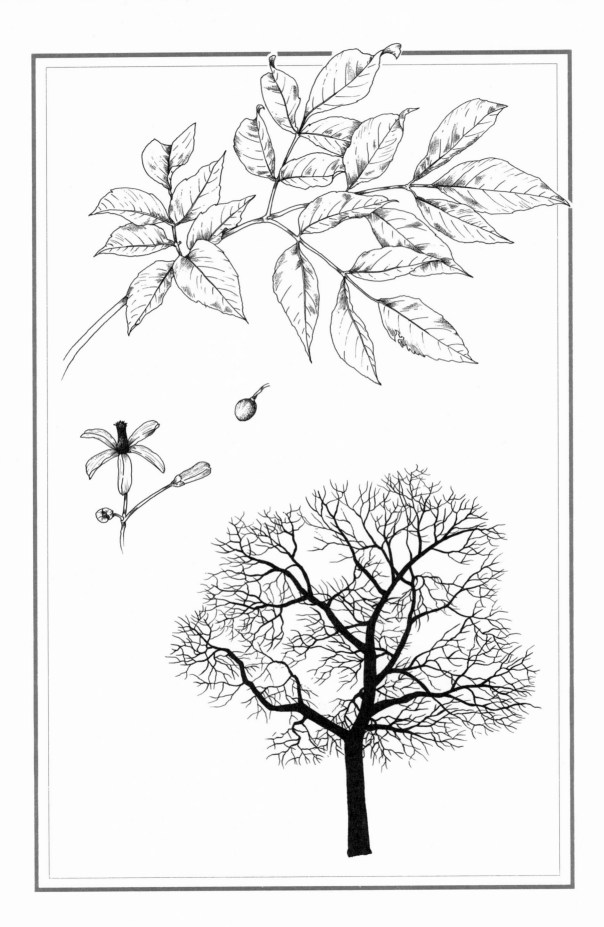

COMMON NAME: *Chinaberry*

BOTANICAL NAME: *Melia azedarach*

FAMILY: Meliaceae (Mahogany)

DESCRIPTION: Chinaberry grows to a height of 50 feet and sometimes spreads an equal distance. The compound leaves are opposite and measure 12 to 24 inches long. The fragrant flowers are lavender or lilac and are borne in long panicles. The round yellow fruit persists after the leaves drop in fall. It is somewhat poisonous.

ORIGIN: Native to the Himalayas and China, chinaberry is now naturalized in many southern states as far north as southern Virginia. It is also naturalized in Hawaii.

HOW TO GROW: Chinaberry grows quickly and is tolerant of pests and disease and extremes of soil conditions, various levels of sunlight, and pollution. Grows in zones 7 to 10.

Other common names for chinaberry include chinatree, Chinese umbrella tree, Pride-of-India, Indian-lilac, Indiana soap plant, soapberry, and Texas umbrella tree. The genus name *Melia*, an ancient Greek name for ash (*Fraxinus*), was given to chinaberry because of the similarity of the foliage. This tree is also known botanically as *M. sempervirens*.

The fruit is considered toxic to poultry, hogs, and humans but seems to be eaten with relish by birds and cattle. Stones from the fruit are sometimes made into beads.

Chinaberry is one of the hardiest members of the Mahogany family. It grows quickly in hot, dry areas and provides welcomed shade. The tree is considered somewhat messy because it seems to be always dropping something—fruit or leaves. It is relatively short-lived.

The soft wood is light reddish tan and attractive, but it is coarse-grained and weak and is not considered durable. The tree is most often grown as an ornamental rather than as a source of lumber. It is, however, sometimes used to make musical instruments.

COMMON NAME: *Cottonwood*
BOTANICAL NAME: *Populus deltoides*
FAMILY: Salicaceae (Willow)

DESCRIPTION: Cottonwood is a very large tree growing to 100 feet tall. The bark is smooth and yellow-green. The trunk often divides into thick branches and opens into a spreading crown. The leaves are as broad as they are long (3 to 6 inches), triangular in shape, and coarsely toothed. They are soft and feltlike underneath. Male and female flowers are borne on separate trees and appear in early spring. Seeds are tiny and cottony, maturing soon after the flowers fade.

ORIGIN: Cottonwoods are found throughout most of the eastern United States and into Canada and can be found at elevations up to 5,000 feet in parts of the West.

HOW TO GROW: Cottonwood is an extremely fast-growing tree, attaining as much as 5 feet per year under favorable conditions. Because the roots grow quickly and are somewhat invasive, these trees are often used for erosion control. In nature this tree is most often found on stream banks or in wet soils. Cottonwoods prefer full sun and well-drained, deep, moist soils but are tolerant of many adverse conditions including salt spray, drought, and air pollution. They are often planted as wind breaks or barriers. Cottonwood is hardy to zone 2.

The name cottonwood comes from the cotton-like seeds that spread with joyous profusion in spring. Another common name, necklace poplar, refers to the seed capsules that are found on a long string, resembling a string of pearls. Still other common names include aspen cottonwood, Carolina poplar, river poplar, water poplar, and yellow cottonwood. The species name *deltoides* means "triangular."

Cottonwood was particularly valuable to early pioneers who used the leaves to feed livestock and treasured the trees for shade and timber. The wood is very light colored and difficult to season well. It is not considered a high-grade wood and today is used to make plywood, matches, and crates. It is also often used in manufacturing boxes because it takes ink for forming letters well.

Cottonwood trees are usually found on cleared fields. Because they are able to withstand flooding, these trees are found on floodplains and in other environments that other trees find intolerable. The roots can withstand saturated water up to a month. In cases of long-term flooding, the trees sometimes actually put forth new root systems on newly deposited silt, sometimes as much as 4 feet above the original roots.

The tolerance of cottonwood in the United States is legendary: Not only will it withstand eastern floods, it will also tolerate western drought. Once established, cottonwoods are astoundingly forgiving to a harsh environment.

Several American Indian tribes from the prairie states considered cottonwood a sacred tree.

Even though the bark of cottonwood contains the substance salicin, similar to aspirin, this tree has not been used extensively for medicine. Tea made from the bark was sometimes drunk to combat scurvy.

Cottonwood is the state tree of Kansas and Nebraska.

COMMON NAME: *Crab Apple, Japanese*

BOTANICAL NAME: *Malus floribunda*

FAMILY: Rosaceae (Rose)

DESCRIPTION: There are approximately twenty-five species in this genus, several of which have great ornamental value. Generally crab apples have alternate leaves measuring 1 to 3 inches long. The flowers, which usually come before the foliage in spring, are pink or bright red or sometimes white, with five rounded petals and fifteen to twenty stamens. The fruit is small and round, usually edible. The cultivated apple, *M. pumilais,* is in this genus as well. Any species in this genus producing fruit less than two inches in diameter is considered a crab apple. Japanese crab apple grows to be 25 feet in height and has attractive dark green leaves. The flowers are pale, pale pink, looking almost white. The fruit is red and yellow. A similar species is Oregon, or Pacific, crab apple, *M. fusca,* a tree growing 30 feet in height with small oblong fruit.

ORIGIN: Crab apples are native to southern Europe and central Asia.

HOW TO GROW: Although crab apples do best when planted from container-grown or balled plants, they are relatively easy to transplant. Good drainage is one of the most important conditions for this tree. It tolerates a wide range of pH in the soil and survives drought admirably when established. The trees should be pruned annually to increase fruit production and to maintain a desirable shape. Grows in zones 4 to 8.

The crab apple is also known as crab tree and garland tree. The wood is hard, heavy, and pinkish to grayish brown in color. The dry weight is 52 pounds per cubic foot. The sapwood is pale and thicker than the heartwood. The wood is difficult to work with but is often used for carving because of its unusually even texture. At one time, it was used extensively to make handsaw handles, to manufacture heads of wooden mallets, and even to make bearings in machinery.

The American Indians used crab-apple wood for making wedges to split other wood.

The fruit, which is small and tart, is used to make jelly and jams. The small apples are also eaten by wildlife, in particular grouse and other birds.

Perhaps because of the tart taste of the fruit, blossoms from the crab apple were considered a symbol of an ill nature.

COMMON NAME: *Crape Myrtle*

BOTANICAL NAME: *Lagerstroemia indica*

FAMILY: Lythraceae (Loosestrife)

DESCRIPTION: Crape myrtle is a graceful spreading tree, with a mature height of about 30 feet and a width of 30 to 40 feet. The light gray bark peels in shreds, exposing the underbark, which is generally a different color. The oblong leaves are 1 to 2 inches long. It is an important ornamental plant, highly prized for its flowers. The blossoms, either white, pink, red, lavender, or purple, appear in clusters during summer. The crinkly blossoms offer an unusual texture. The variety 'Muskogee' grows over 20 feet high and spreads 15 feet. Pale lavender flowers appear in summer, and the leaves turn bright red in fall. 'Natchez', which grows as wide as it does tall, has white flowers and leaves that turn orange and red in autumn.

ORIGIN: China and southeast Asia

HOW TO GROW: Crape myrtle, needing full sun, does not bloom well in shady areas. It tolerates drought conditions once it is established but needs plenty of moisture when young. This small tree prefers well-drained, slightly acidic soils. Grows in zones 7 to 9.

Crape myrtle was named by Linnaeus for his Swedish friend Magnus von Lagerstroem (1696–1759). The common name refers to the petals, which appear wrinkled, like crepe paper. It has no relation to the true myrtle.

Also called "lilac of the South," crape myrtle is good for creating avenues. Because the flowers appear on shoots of the current year's growth, these satisfactory plants bloom freely even when pruned. So adaptable are the shrubs that they are even lovely when grown in large

tubs or containers for patios and terraces.

Crape myrtle can be used either as a specimen plant or as a hedge or screen. The latter provides an excellent place to grow ground covers that need full sun in early spring but like a little shade during the summer months when the tree is foliated.

Plant breeders have developed dwarf varieties, more disease-resistant varieties, and cultivars that can withstand colder temperatures.

COMMON NAME: *Cypress, Leyland*

BOTANICAL NAME: *Cupressocyparis leylandii*

FAMILY: Cupressaceae (Cypress)

DESCRIPTION: Leyland cypress is a tall, narrow tree growing to a height of 100 feet or more, spreading only about 20 feet at maturity. The leaves are blue-green, flat, and scalelike as opposed to needlelike. The small cones are ½ inch long. Different cultivars have slightly different colored foliage. 'Leighton Green' has gray-green leaves, 'Naylor's Blue' has a decided blue tint to it, and 'Castewellan' appears yellow.

ORIGIN: garden of C. J. Leyland in Welshpool, England

HOW TO GROW: Leyland cypress grows in all but extreme conditions, including salt air. It does not like overly soggy, poorly drained soils or very dry conditions or highly alkaline conditions. Plant from container-grown plants in full sun. Grows in zones 7 to 10.

The genus name, *Cupressocyparis,* originates from two Greek words, *kus* meaning "to produce" and *parisos* meaning "equal." This refers to the beautifully symmetrical growth patterns of several cypress species.

Leyland cypress is good for hedging because it withstands heavy pruning. Within a period of about twenty-five years, it can grow 50 to 60 feet.

Cypress is one of the four woods thought to have been made into the cross on which Jesus was crucified. One early poet wrote of these trees:

Nailed were His feet to Cedar, to Palm His hands,
Cypress His body bore, title on Olive stands.

Because the cypress will not grow again once it has been cut, it was used by the ancient Romans as a symbol of the permanency of death. In old England cypress garlands were worn by the genteel class at funerals.

Mediterranean cypress is particularly strong and long lasting. The gates of Constantinople are made from this wood. It was also used to make sea chests.

COMMON NAME: *Daphne*

BOTANICAL NAME: *Daphne* x Burkwoodii

FAMILY: Thymelaeaceae (Mezereum)

DESCRIPTION: This well-known low-growing shrub is a cross between *D. caucasica* and *D. Cneorum.* It is considered partially evergreen and has narrow linear leaves. The blossoms are white tinged with pink and occur in terminal heads surrounded by leaves. The best-known cultivar is 'Somerset', a broad, low, compact version of the species. Both the species and the cultivar are free flowering and have attractive red fruits. *D. Cneorum,* garland flower, is evergreen.

ORIGIN: Alps and northern Italy

HOW TO GROW: Once established, daphnes do not like to be moved. Choose a site carefully for daphne plants, and when planted, leave them alone. Young container-grown plants usually survive longer and are quicker to establish than older plants. Mulching with a mixture of limestone grit and leaf mold seems to be beneficial to the plants. Although regular pruning is not necessary, occasionally long twigs will stray out from the bush and should be trimmed. This species of daphne is hardy to New England.

According to Greek myth, Daphne was a lovely young nymph who spent her days happily playing in the woods. One day while she was dancing in happy innocence, she was seen by the Greek god Apollo. Apollo immediately fell in love with the young nymph and pursued her with great fervor, determined to win her affections. Daphne wanted nothing to do with Apollo and finally prayed to the other gods for help. Unable to stop Apollo, the other gods could only help by turning Daphne into a laurel bush.

Although Apollo was crushed, he always considered this bush sacred. *Daphne* is the Greek word for laurel.

The blossoms of daphne are incredibly sweet-scented.

Daphne means "painting the lily" according to the English language of flowers, presumably meaning that the daphne is as lovely as the lily flower. According to another English book on folklore, daphne means "desire to please."

COMMON NAME: *Dogwood, Flowering*
BOTANICAL NAME: *Cornus florida*
FAMILY: Cornaceae (Dogwood)

DESCRIPTION: Dogwood trees do not grow very tall, usually only about 30 feet, and they often spread as wide as they are tall. These trees are spectacularly beautiful in spring when in bloom. The flowers are small green nuggets set in among four large white petallike bracts. A red or pink cultivar, 'Rubra', is also available through the nursery trade. The leaves are oval, 3 to 5 inches long, and deeply veined. Autumn foliage is red or purplish red. The fruit turns bright scarlet and persists throughout the winter. Japanese dogwood, *C. kousa*, does not grow as tall, blooms a little later, and has pointed bracts.

ORIGIN: eastern United States

HOW TO GROW: Dogwoods are relatively easy to grow, requiring only ordinary garden soil and sun or partial shade. It is a border tree, occurring naturally at the forest edge. A blight affecting dogwood trees has greatly depleted natural populations of this tree over the past decade, particularly in the northeastern states. Grows in zones 6 to 9.

Dogwood has been loved and cherished in this country for many centuries. Native Americans took the arrival of the white flowers as a signal that it was time to plant crops. The bark was boiled in water and made into an extract to soothe sore muscles. Tea made from the bark was used to induce sweating to break a fever. During the Civil War when quinine was often in short supply for soldiers, dogwood tea served as a poor substitute.

The Pacific dogwood, *C. nuttallii*, was also used medicinally. The story is told of Townsend, a physician who lived at Fort Vancouver. He was called in to treat two Cowlitz Indian children who were suffering from fever. Having no quinine, he substituted a concoction made from the bark of the Pacific dogwood and had very satisfying results. In addition to its use as a medicine, dogwood tea was taken as an appetite stimulant. This species was named by James

Audubon for his good friend Thomas Nuttall, a botanist and an explorer.

The bright red berries were sometimes soaked in brandy and were taken to relieve excessive stomach acid. Fresh twigs were chewed, which served as a primitive toothbrush. (After being chewed for a few minutes, the fibers at the ends of the twig separate and become soft, forming a brush.)

The wood of this tree is extraordinarily hard and is used for making items such as weaving shuttles and golf-club heads. According to the English language of flowers, dogwood means durability.

According to legend the dogwood tree at one time was as tall and mighty as the oak. Because of the strength of the wood, it was chosen to make the cross on which Jesus Christ was crucified. The dogwood was so ashamed of its task, the story goes, that it begged Jesus for forgiveness. In His compassion for all living things, Jesus took pity on the dogwood and decreed that from then on the tree would be slender and twisted so that it would never again be used as a cross. As a reminder of its history, however, the dogwood tree would also bear blossoms in the shape of a cross. In the center of the blossom would appear a crown of thorns, and each petal would carry at its outer edge nail prints stained with red.

Dogwood is the state tree of Virginia.

COMMON NAME: *Elm, Smoothleaf*
BOTANICAL NAME: *Ulmus carpinifolia*
FAMILY: Ulmaceae (Elm)

DESCRIPTION: The leaves of smoothleaf elm are smooth and shiny on both sides. The flowers and fruit are small and inconspicuous. The tree grows to a height of 70 to 75 feet at maturity. *U. parvifolia*, Chinese or lacebark elm, is a shorter tree, usually not growing higher than 60 feet. The bark comes off in sheets, often creating interesting patterns on the trunk, thus the name lacebark. Leaves turn yellow or purplish in fall.

ORIGIN: Smoothleaf elm is native to Eurasia and northern Africa. Chinese elm is native to eastern Asia.

HOW TO GROW: American elms were once planted along city streets throughout New England and the Midwest. These trees were hard hit in 1927 by the Dutch elm disease, and most were killed. Other species of elms and resistant strains of the American elm have been developed that are not as susceptible to this deadly disease. Elms are easy to transplant and do well in sunny areas with rich, well-drained soil. They make very good shade trees, allowing dappled sunlight to filter through to the ground. Smoothleaf elm grows in zones 5 to 8. Chinese elm grows in zones 5 to 10.

The common name slippery elm (*U. rubra*) was given to this tree because when the inner bark mixes with water, the fibers swell and create a slippery, soothing substance. This substance was made into an ointment to heal burns and alleviate skin disorders. Native American healers, who showed the early colonists the benefits of this herb, also made a concoction from the bark to treat stomach and kidney disorders.

Folk healers have long used slippery elm tea to treat young children and infants. Modern research has found that chemicals within this bark contain substances that soothe and soften the skin.

The American elm is the state tree of Massachusetts and North Dakota.

COMMON NAME: *Eucalyptus*
BOTANICAL NAME: *Eucalyptus globulus*
FAMILY: Myrtaceae (Myrtle)

DESCRIPTION: *Eucalyptus globulus,* or bluegum eucalyptus, is the most extensively cultivated eucalyptus in the world. It grows to a height of 120 feet and has narrow, lance-shaped evergreen leaves. The most outstanding characteristic of this tree is its fragrant blue-green foliage.

ORIGIN: Victoria and Tasmania

HOW TO GROW: Eucalyptus prefers dry soil and full, hot sun. Until they are established, the trees must be treated carefully in fall. They should be supplied with plenty of water and tender loving care, and water and fertilizer should be cut back drastically to harden the roots off for winter. It is hardy only to zone 9.

Eucalyptus is an enormous genus composed of 522 different species. Other names for the common eucalyptus include Eucalypt, Australian gum, gum tree, ironbark, and stringybark.

The name eucalyptus is derived from two Greek words, *eu,* meaning "well," and *kalyptos,* meaning "covered." *Kalyptos* refers to the lid that covers the flowering bud.

E. cinerea is the tallest known tree. One species averages 300 feet in height, and the lowest branches are 180 feet off the ground. Eucalyptus puts out a tremendous network of roots. It grows well in swampy areas where the roots take up so much water that they actually drain the area. This characteristic was put to good advantage during the late nineteenth century when the tree was planted in swamps infested with malaria-carrying mosquitoes. The trees quickly drained the areas, creating a drier, healthier environment.

The highly aromatic oil found in eucalyptus leaves is often mixed with water to create a steam bath helpful in treating respiratory ailments. Eucalyptus oil is also good for treating rough, chapped skin and dandruff.

The fast-growing bluegum eucalyptus is good for screens or windbreaks. The wood is used for fuel and in making fiberboard, pulp, thatch, and even perfume.

Eucalyptus was first discovered by the first Englishman to reach Australia, William Dampier. Dampier was an author, a botanist, an expert hydrographer, and a navigator. The tree was then introduced to the United States through California in 1853. More than fifty different species are grown in the United States, over 80 percent of which are bluegum.

In Australia local inhabitants would break off pieces from the great eucalyptus tree and suck the water out of them to quench their thirst. The dried root was pounded into meal, and the seeds were eaten. Eucalyptus seeds were also sometimes used to make rosaries.

COMMON NAME: *Fig, Benjamin*
BOTANICAL NAME: *Ficus benjamina*
FAMILY: Moraceae (Mulberry)

DESCRIPTION: There are more than 800 species of evergreen trees, shrubs, and vines in the genus *Ficus*. Benjamin fig is grown outdoors in frost-free areas and is quite common as a houseplant in other areas. Outdoors it grows to a height of about 40 feet and has graceful, spreading branches. The attractive dark green leaves are leathery, evergreen, and oblong, measuring 2 to 4 inches long. Both the flowers and the fruit are relatively inconspicuous. Grows outdoors in zones 9 and 10. *F. elastica* 'Decora', rubber plant, is another species in this genus of ornamental value as both a houseplant and a garden plant in appropriate areas. In its native tropical habitat, rubber plant grows to be a very large tree. The green and shiny leaves are 6 to 12 inches long.

ORIGIN: Benjamin fig is native to Indo-Malaysia; the rubber plant is native from Nepal to Assam.

HOW TO GROW: Both indoors and out, Benjamin fig needs evenly moist but not wet soils and responds well to fertilizing 2 to 3 times a year. It prefers full sun and should not be overwatered. The rubber plant is very tolerant of abuse and neglect. It tolerates low light, drought, and low humidity.

The word *fig* comes from the Latin word for fig, *ficus*. Ficus is from an ancient Hebrew word, *feg*, meaning "to spread out" and refers to the growing habit of this small tree. *F. carica*, native to Caria in Asia Minor, is thought to be the original parent of many of today's cultivars.

Fig trees bear numerous small unisexual male, female, and gall flowers. The flowers are organized to provide breeding and mating areas for aganoid wasps. The larvae feed on the nutritious ovary walls.

According to Greek legend Sykeus and his mother, Ge, were pursued by Zeus during the war of the Titans. So fierce was the pursuit of Zeus that finally, in desperation, Ge turned Sykeus into a fig tree. As he changed, Sykeus was struck by a bolt of lightning sent from Zeus;

therefore, the fig is thought to carry the power of Zeus.

Yet another legend about the fig says that the goddess Demeter first revealed to mortals the fruit of autumn by showing them the fig. She did this to reward King Phytalus, who had received her in his home.

According to an old Greek superstition, a priestess could tame and lead to the sacrificial altar any bull, no matter how wild, by tying a branch of wild fig around his neck.

Romans thought that it was the god Bacchus who introduced the fig to mankind. For this reason figs were considered sacred, and the gods were often shown carrying branches of figs.

Figs were also important to the early Christians, and soon the fig became symbolic of security and a happy family life. In the Bible, in Genesis 3:7, it is written that Adam and Eve "sewed fig leaves together, and made themselves aprons."

In parts of England fig pies were served on special Sundays during Lent, usually the Sun-

day before Easter. Also called "Figpie Wake," this ritual commemorated the day when Jesus desired to eat figs along the road to Bethany.

In the Orient figs are symbols of fertility and propagation.

COMMON NAME: *Fir, Douglas*

BOTANICAL NAME: *Pseudotsuga menzieseii*

FAMILY: Pinaceae (Pine)

DESCRIPTION: Douglas fir is valuable as a Christmas tree, for its lumber, and for its ornamental value. Although it grows only 40 to 60 feet tall in cultivation, in its native habitat this tree sometimes reaches a height of 200 feet or more. The leaves are needlelike, 1 to 1½ inches long, and blunt on the end. Underneath they appear to have white bands, and on the upper sides they are dark green. The cones, which are 2 to 4 inches long, are purplish when they first appear and then turn yellow as they mature. Douglas fir differs from the true fir by having cones that hang down like those of pine and spruce. *P. menzieseii* var. 'glauca' is a hardy variety, suitable for growing in the Midwest and Northeast. This variety is sometimes hardy even into zone 3.

ORIGIN: Pacific Coast

HOW TO GROW: In spite of its magnificent growth, Douglas fir has a relatively shallow root system and is easily uprooted. Plant in well-drained moist soil that is, for best results, slightly acidic. It is particularly sensitive to dryness caused by high summer temperatures or winds or insufficiently moist soils. Deep mulching proves to be most beneficial. It can be grown successfully in zones 4 to 6.

The Douglas fir was named for David Douglas (1798–1834), a botanist from Scotland who was sent by the Royal Horticultural Society to the United States to collect plants. In 1825 he traveled to Hudson Bay and on this journey discovered the Douglas fir.

P. menzieseii is a great timber species and is ranked first in the United States in total volume of timber in lumber production.

The quality of the wood from this tree varies tremendously, depending on where it is found. The yellow or light tan wood is medium-hard,

strong, and heavy. Growth rings are easily identified in the split wood.

Douglas fir was used to lay thousands of miles of railroad tracks in the West. The lumber was also made into telegraph and telephone poles. The bark was ground into a substance used as a soil conditioner and also as an absorbent filler in acoustical products. The bark was sometimes used as a cork substitute for such items as the soles of shoes.

During World War II soldiers' footlockers, almost without exception, were made from Douglas fir.

The introduction of plywood changed forever the wood industry, and Douglas fir was the primary choice for its production.

Individual needles of this species remain on the tree for three to five years. Continuous new growth makes the tree evergreen. Deer and elk graze on the foliage; birds and small mammals eat the seeds.

Douglas fir is the state tree of Oregon.

COMMON NAME: *Franklinia*

BOTANICAL NAME: *Franklinia alatamaha*

FAMILY: Theaceae (Tea)

DESCRIPTION: This startlingly beautiful tree grows 10 to 30 feet tall and has lovely large white blossoms that measure 3 inches across. Each flower is composed of a five-lobed silky-haired calyx, five petals, and many conspicuous yellow stamens. Each individual flower resembles a single camellia blossom. Flowers appear in late summer and fall. The tree has multiple trunks and gracefully spreading branches. The shiny green foliage turns red or orange in autumn.

ORIGIN: Franklinia is native to southeastern Georgia, now known only in cultivation.

HOW TO GROW: Franklinia needs full sun and moist, acidic soil rich in organic matter. It makes a beautiful accent tree. It grows in zones 6 to 8 and is hardy to southern New England. This tree can be propagated by seeds, cuttings, and layering in early spring.

Franklinia was named for Benjamin Franklin, who died in 1790. It is also known as *Gordonia alatamaha*. This is the only known species in this genus.

The story of Franklinia is a cherished one in botanical circles because it portrays so well the essential importance of plant collection and documentation. Franklinia was first discovered by the well-known botanists and plant explorers John Bartram and his son, William. They found this beautiful tree growing near Fort Barrington, close to the mouth of the Altamaha River in Georgia, in 1765 while on a plant exploration trip.

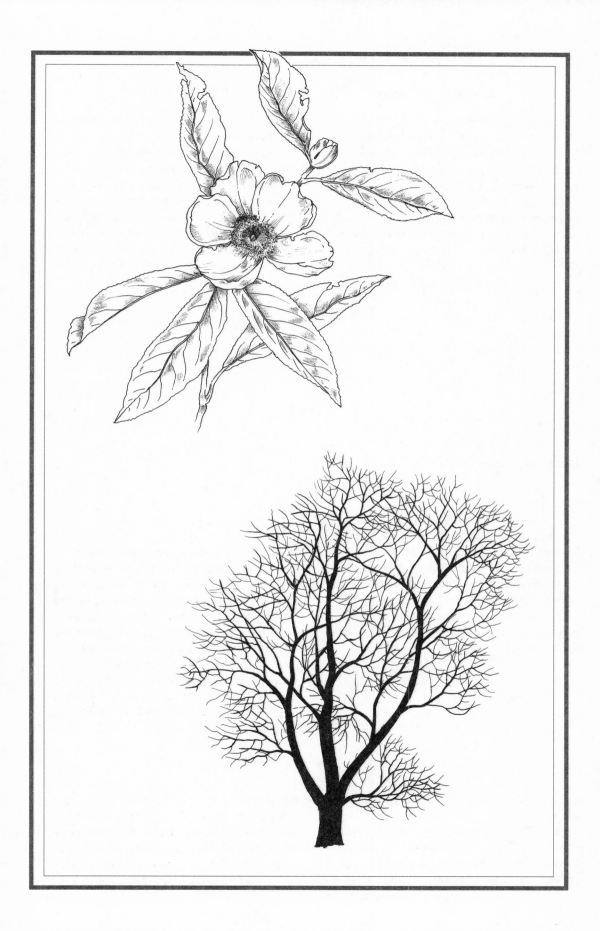

On a return trip to the South in 1773, William Bartram spotted this tree again and took the time to collect small seedlings and seeds from the tree. His fortuitous action saved the tree from possible extinction.

The tree was obviously rare, and as far as anyone could determine, grew only in a specific locale. The last recorded sighting in the wild was in 1803 when John Lyon, a plant hunter and nurseryman, found a few specimens growing within a ½-acre area near the site of the old Fort Barrington.

Luckily the tree is relatively easy to propagate, and Bartram managed to grow Franklinia in his garden in Philadelphia. Today the tree is grown often in cultivation in many parts of the East. All known plants are from Bartram's original collection, linking past and present and making all gardeners who grow this tree feel as if they truly have a part of Bartram's garden.

COMMON NAME: *Gardenia*

BOTANICAL NAME: *Gardenia jasminoides*

FAMILY: Rubiaceae (Madder)

DESCRIPTION: This small evergreen shrub grows 2 to 5 feet tall and has shiny, thick, leathery leaves measuring 2 to 4 inches long. The blossoms are beautiful and highly fragrant white flowers that appear in early spring and last through summer. The shrubs have a neat, compact growth, making them desirable for accent plants or in hedges. Cultivars have been developed varying in height and flower size.

ORIGIN: China

HOW TO GROW: Gardenias grow in zones 8 to 10 but can be grown in colder areas in containers, which must be moved indoors when the weather turns cool. These shrubs need to be grown in full sun in cool areas but should be planted where they receive some protection from the sun in hot and humid areas. They prefer moist, rich, acidic soil and should be mulched annually to protect the shallow roots. They are heavy feeders during blooming period. Most gardenia cultivars should be spaced about 3 feet apart.

The gardenia shrub is also known as cape jasmine.

The genus name, *Gardenia,* was chosen in honor of Alexander Garden of Charleston, South Carolina. Garden was an outstanding botanist and often corresponded with Linnaeus, sending him many unusual plants from the New World including the magnolia. During the American Revolution Garden was guided by his Tory sympathies and returned to England, where he was eventually elected a Fellow of the Royal Society.

Ho Hsien-Ku, the Chinese goddess of flow-

ers, decreed that reverence should be paid to a special flower each month of the year. According to the Chinese floral calendar, gardenia is the flower for the month of November.

The blossom of gardenia is almost overpoweringly fragrant. The scent is frequently used in the perfume industry and brings to mind hot, sultry nights in the deep South.

COMMON NAME: *Ginkgo*

BOTANICAL NAME: *Ginkgo biloba*

FAMILY: Ginkgoaceae (Ginkgo)

DESCRIPTION: The most distinguishing feature of the ginkgo tree is its small and fan-shaped leaf. The leaves resemble a frond of the maidenhair fern, thus the common name maidenhair-tree. At maturity the gingko grows to be 125 feet tall. In autumn the leaves turn a soft yellow and then fall all at once. The fruit, which appears on the female tree, has a decidedly unpleasant odor.

ORIGIN: China

HOW TO GROW: Because the fruit is so foul smelling, only male trees should be planted. The trees must be planted in full sun. They are tolerant of a wide range of environmental conditions, including city pollution, and are relatively pest free. Gingkoes grow in zones 5 to 8.

Ginkgoes are considered the oldest cultivated tree on earth. Ginkgoes are sometimes called living fossils because they are extinct in the wild and are only found growing in cultivation. *G. biloba* is the only genus and species in this family, dating back to the Permian period of the Paleozoic era, 225 to 280 million years ago. Two genera, Ginkgoites and Baiera, are known only from fossilized leaves. All cultivated specimens are from trees that originally grew around Chinese temples.

In spite of its interesting historical beginnings, ginkgo trees have earned the not-so-pleasant name of "stink bomb tree." The "stink" refers to the unpleasantly scented fruit of the tree.

Although the fruit itself is putrid, within this flesh is found an edible kernel, which is included in much Oriental cooking. Many Oriental rites include the use of these kernels, which are called silvery apricots. The name ginkgo in Chinese means "white nut."

Ginkgoes are often planted in urban areas because of their tolerance to smoke, pollution, and dust. The trees also grow in poor, compact soils. In spite of its adaptability, ginkgo is now found only in cultivation; nowhere does it occur in the wild.

A ginkgo tree found in Kew Gardens in London was supposedly planted by an English princess in 1759.

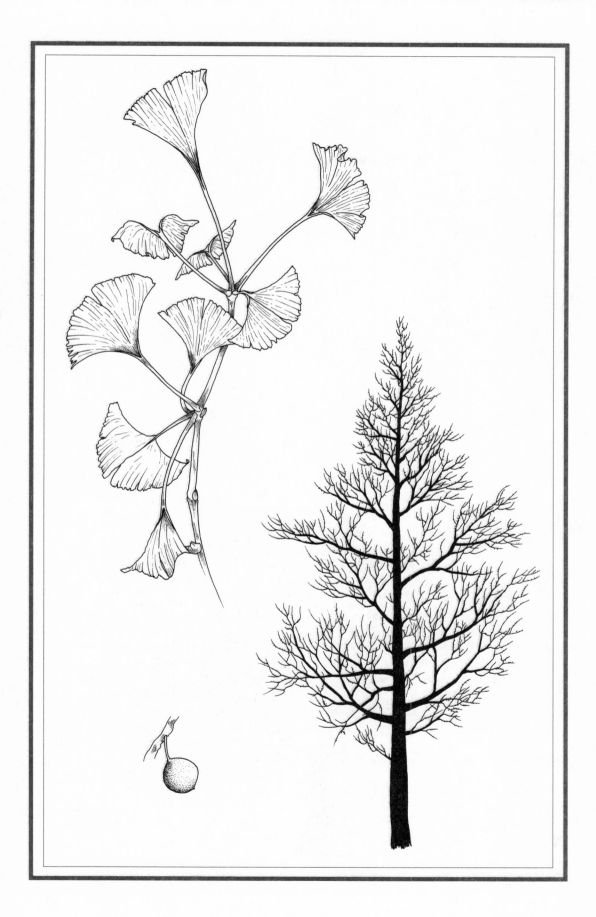

COMMON NAME: *Golden Rain Tree*

BOTANICAL NAME: *Koelreuteria paniculata*

FAMILY: Sapindaceae (Soapberry)

DESCRIPTION: Golden rain tree is named for its summer bloom of yellow flowers, which cover the tree. The attractive, 10- to 18-inch-long leaves are composed of seven to fifteen leaflets, which resemble fern fronds. The tree reaches a height of just 40 feet. The seeds occur in 2-inch-long brightly colored papery pods.

ORIGIN: eastern Asia, China, Korea, and Japan

HOW TO GROW: Golden rain trees should be grown in full sun. They tolerate a variety of soil conditions and seem unaffected by air pollution. Young trees benefit from staking and pruning, which increases branching, and regular watering, which helps establish a strong root system. The trees put forth deep roots. Can be grown in zones 5 to 8.

Golden rain tree, also called China tree, pride of India, and varnish tree, is one of the earliest cultivated trees in China, where since ancient times it has been known as *luan*. Three thousand years ago in an early Chinese dynasty, it was designated as one of the five official memorial trees. It was often planted on tombs of scholars. The Chinese make necklaces from the attractive seeds.

Pierre D'Incarville introduced the golden rain tree to Europe in 1763. The genus name commemorates Joseph Gottlieb Koelreuter, professor of natural history at Karlsruhe, Germany, in the late eighteenth century.

The flowers make an attractive yellow dye and are sometimes used for medicines. In Fiji, the leaves of *K. elegans* were boiled to produce a black hair dye.

In the United States golden rain tree is beloved as well. Every year in New Harmony, Indiana, the townspeople hold the Golden Rain Tree Festival during the summer months when the tree is in bloom.

COMMON NAME: *Hackberry*

BOTANICAL NAME: *Celtis occidentalis*

FAMILY: Ulmaceae (Elm)

DESCRIPTION: This species of hackberry grows to a height of 120 feet. The leaves are 5 inches long and are shiny green on top and paler green underneath. The sweet fruit is orange-red to dark purple.

ORIGIN: Hackberry grows from Quebec south to North Carolina and Alabama.

HOW TO GROW: In nature hackberry is found along stream banks or in canyons and valleys. In cultivation it needs constant moisture but is not particular as to soil type. It can be propagated by seed or by stem cuttings in early spring. It is hardy to zone 5.

The name hackberry originates probably from the Scottish name "hagberry" meaning marsh berry, a Scottish name for a cherry. Witches' brooms is another name given to this plant because mites and fungi often cause deformed growth on the branches, making them appear gnarled and twisted as a witch's broom might look. Other names for this tree are sugarberry and nettletree.

Daniel Harmon Brush wrote in his book *Growing Up with Southern Illinois*, "The floors of the cabins were made of puncheons split as thin as desired from hunks of the hackberry tree, a very free-splitting wood of firm and beautiful grain, and white in color."

In spite of this favorable report of the wood of this tree, hackberry lumber is not known for its beauty. The tough, flexible wood is used to make such mundane items as inexpensive furniture, fence posts, kitchen cabinets, crates, and boxes.

American Indians flavored their food with the berries. Many kinds of wildlife and birds, including quail, woodpeckers, and cedar waxwings, enjoy the fruit of this tree.

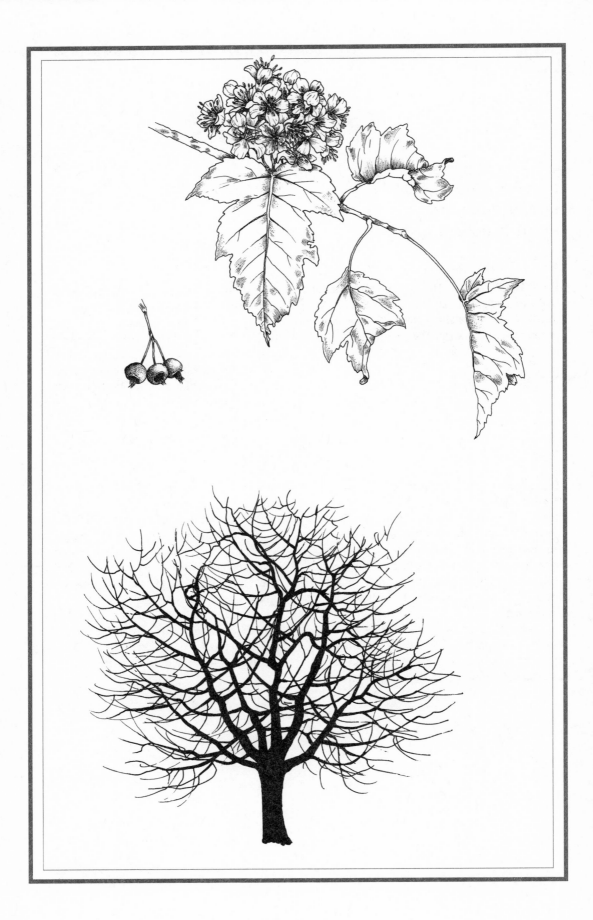

COMMON NAME: *Hawthorn, Washington*

BOTANICAL NAME: *Crataegus phaenopyrum*

FAMILY: Rosaceae (Rose)

DESCRIPTION: There are more than 1,000 species in the hawthorn genus, many of which are commonly found in eastern United States. Few of these are desirable ornamentally, but one of the best species to use in the garden is Washington hawthorn. This tree grows to be 30 feet tall and has dense growth with thin 3-inch-long thorns. The leaves are triangular in shape and have 3 to 7 lobes. In autumn the fruit is bright scarlet and covers the tree; the leaves turn a lovely reddish orange.

ORIGIN: Pennsylvania to Florida

HOW TO GROW: Washington hawthorn is one of the most trouble-free of all the hawthorns. It grows in ordinary garden soil but prefers alkaline soils and open spaces. Hawthorns are often used as barriers because of their thorns, but unfortunately they do not lend themselves well to being clipped as a hedge. Grows in zones 5 to 9.

Washington hawthorn was introduced to Pennsylvania from Washington, D.C., in the early nineteenth century. Because of its point of origin and the prominent protrusions on the plant, it was referred to as "Washington-thorn."

English hawthorn, *C. monogyna*, has much history and folklore associated with it. An old English proverb says, "Cleave to thy Crown, though it hang on a bush." It refers to a legend concerning Henry VII, who was crowned king of England in 1485. The story is that when Richard III was slain in battle, his battle crown was found near a hawthorn bush. From that time forward the hawthorn became a lucky symbol for Henry VII.

In France Norman peasants wore sprigs of hawthorn in their caps. This custom illustrated their belief that Christ's crown of thorns was made from a hawthorn bush. According to the English language of flowers, hawthorn is a symbol of hope.

Hawthorn has been used medicinally by the ancient Greeks, American Indians, and the Chinese. The fruits and flowers were used to treat heart problems. Scientific studies indicate that substances from this plant reduce blood pressure and act as an effective heart tonic.

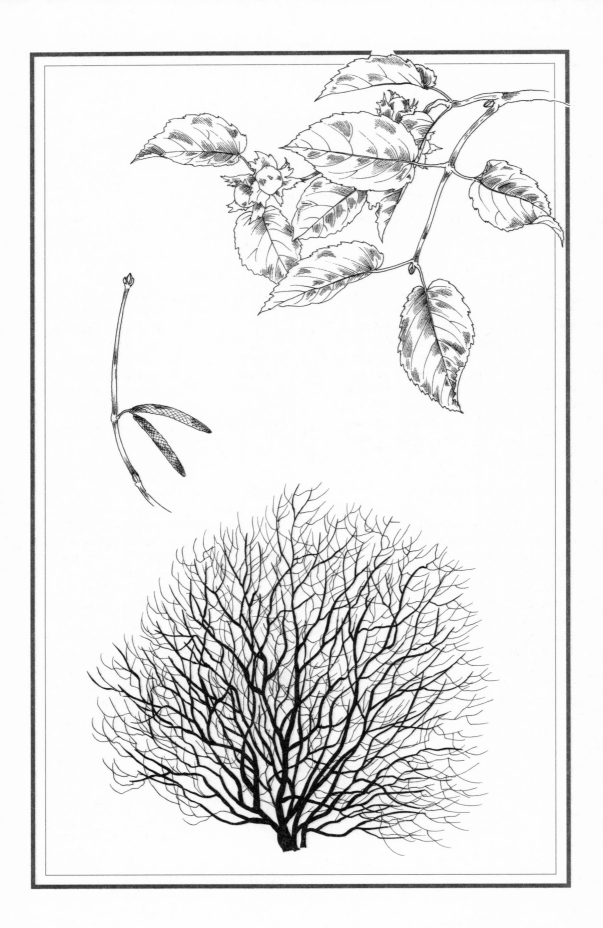

COMMON NAME: *Hazelnut, American*
BOTANICAL NAME: *Corylus americana*
FAMILY: Betulaceae (Birch)

DESCRIPTION: American hazelnut grows only about 10 feet tall. The leaves are large, heart-shaped, and irregularly toothed. Both the stems and leafstalks have prominent hairs. The fruits are found in leafy husks. *C. colurna*, Turkish filbert, is a closely related species. It is an attractive pyramidal-shaped tree growing 50 feet tall. The bark is corky and rough. Turkish filbert is generally grown for its delicious nuts.

ORIGIN: American hazelnut is native from Maine to Georgia, west to Missouri and Oklahoma.

HOW TO GROW: Grow in rich, well-drained soil in full sun or partial shade. Turkish filbert tolerates drought well and seems unaffected by hot summers and cold winters. Grows in zones 4 to 7.

Hairs from the twigs of this species were thought to hold the capability of expelling worms. European folk healers through the ages as well as American Indians have used hazelnut hairs for this purpose. The Indians also made tea from the bark, which they found useful in treating hives and in breaking a fever. Wounds and sores were treated with a poultice made from the bark, which was thought to be particularly effective in closing cuts.

COMMON NAME: *Heather, Scotch*
BOTANICAL NAME: *Calluna vulgaris*
FAMILY: Ericaceae (Heath)

DESCRIPTION: Scotch heather generally grows to a height of 2 feet and spreads 2 to 4 feet wide. It is an evergreen shrub, which blooms during late summer and fall. The flowers are usually pink or purple and are found clustered together at the ends of branches. The cultivar 'Spring Torch' is only 12 inches tall. It has bright yellow foliage in early spring and turns bright red in autumn.

ORIGIN: Europe and Asia Minor

HOW TO GROW: Heather is useful as a ground cover. It is tolerant to salt spray and grows well in sandy soils, making it beneficial in a seaside garden. It does need full sun and moist, acidic, well-drained soil. Pruning after flowering in spring keeps a neat, compact growth form. Because the roots are shallow, they should be mulched and then should not be disturbed. Plant in fall or early spring. Most cultivars should be spaced 3 feet apart. Grows in zones 4 to 7.

Heather covers the moors and heaths of Scotland and is affectionately called "bonnie blooming heather."

The name heather is derived from the ancient Middle English word *hadder* or perhaps from the Norse word *height*. The genus name *Calluna* comes from a Greek word meaning "to brush or sweep," which refers to the custom of tying branches of heather together to make brooms.

Although purple heather is quite common throughout the highlands of Scotland, white heather is somewhat rare and consequently is considered a symbol of good luck.

Highlanders used stacks of heather mixed with mud and straw to build walls and thatch roofs for their small cabins. The sweet-smelling heather was also used to make temporary mattresses and bedding.

COMMON NAME: *Hemlock*

BOTANICAL NAME: *Tsuga canadensis*

FAMILY: Pinaceae (Pine)

DESCRIPTION: Hemlocks are evergreen trees with needlelike leaves. They grow 30 to 70 feet tall. *T. canadensis*, Eastern (or Canada) hemlock, has a forked trunk, growing 40 to 70 feet tall in cultivation (taller in the wild). Cones are ½ to 1 inch long. *T. heterophylla*, western hemlock, grows well on the Pacific coast but not in the East. In its natural habitat western hemlock may reach 200 feet in height.

ORIGIN: Eastern (Canada) hemlock is native to eastern United States. Western hemlock is native from Alaska south to California.

HOW TO GROW: Hemlocks need moist acidic soils, partial shade, and protection from drying winds. Hemlocks are often grown together to form a screen or windblock. They really prefer a moist, cool environment but with adaptations grow in zones 4 to 7.

The wood from the western hemlock is strong with straight grains. It is free of pitch, saws off easily, and is easily worked. It was used primarily for studding and for making ladders. Floors, also, were often made from hemlock because it takes a good polish and darkens with age. Today the greatest use of western hemlock is for making paper, the largest percentage going into newsprint.

In Henry Wadsworth Longfellow's poem "Evangeline," he wrote of "the forest primeval, the murmuring pines and the hemlock."

Hemlocks are often the biggest trees in the forest because of their tolerance to shade and the ability of the seeds to germinate in the duff of a pine-forest soil.

Hemlock branches were included in steam baths, which were designed to help heal rheumatism, colds, and coughs. These "sweat lodges" also helped to induce sweating to break a fever.

Colds and pain associated with fever, coughs, and digestive disorders were treated with tea made from the inner bark. A wash was made from the bark, which was used externally to help stop bleeding. Western hemlock supplies alpha cellulose for the manufacture of cellophane, rayon yarns, and plastics.

Alaskan Indians made bread from the inner bark.

Poison hemlock, *Conium maculatum*, is a different plant altogether. It is a herbaceous plant rather than a tree. All parts of it are poisonous. Care should be exercised because poison hemlock closely resembles the common and harmless Queen Anne's lace.

Eastern, or Canada, hemlock is the state tree of Pennsylvania. Western hemlock is the state tree of Washington.

COMMON NAME: *Hickory, Bitternut*
BOTANICAL NAME: *Carya cordiformis*
FAMILY: Juglandaceae (Hickory)

DESCRIPTION: Bitternut hickory grows to a height of 60 to 80 feet. The leaves are alternate and pinnately compound, measuring 6 to 10 inches long. The light brown or gray bark has shallow furrows, and the flowers are small, appearing in early spring. The fruit is a nut, which, in this species, is quite bitter. *C. illinoiensis* is the familiar pecan, which grows 70 to 100 feet tall and has delicious reddish brown nuts. The leaves are long, 9 to 20 inches, and are composed of nine to eleven leaflets. *C. ovata*, shagbark hickory, has gray bark that peels in long strips. The leaves turn yellow in fall. Other species include *C. glabra*, pignut hickory, and *C. tomentosa*, mockernut hickory.

ORIGIN: Quebec to Florida and Louisiana. The largest stands are in the lower Mississippi Valley region.

HOW TO GROW: Hickory and pecan trees need full sun and moist, rich, well-drained soil. Different species grow in zones 4 to 9.

Hickory heartwood is very hard and heavy, averaging 42 to 52 pounds per cubic foot. It has an unusual combination of strength, toughness, hardness, and stiffness and a high degree of shrinkage. It should be dried carefully.

Hickory is prized for its value as firewood and in making charcoal. Pignut hickory, also called smoothbark hickory, is currently used to make skis and tool handles. Eighty percent of hickory wood is used to make tool handles.

In days past the wood was used to make wagon wheels and picker sticks for the textile industry because of its ability to withstand great vibrations. The common name pignut was given during colonial days when hogs ate the nuts with great relish.

American Indians extracted oil from butternut hickory nuts to use in ceremonial rituals. The husks were used to make a yellow or brown dye.

The most economically important hickory is shagbark, *C. ovata*, which grows from northeastern United States to southwestern Mexico. Veneers, skis, molding, and bent plywood are made from the very strong wood.

Pecans, closely related to hickories, are considered one of the most valuable cultivated native American trees. Not only are the nuts economically important, the lumber is used to make furniture, flooring, and veneer. Although the lumber is desirable, it is in short supply because the tree grows with a short trunk and twisted branches, making much of it unusable. Pecan wood is also used in smoking meat.

Pecans were named for the Algonquin Indian Peccan. The Indians believed that this tree was a part of the Great Spirit. The species name *illinoiensis* means "Illinois nuts," suggesting that the trees were found at least as far north as the state of Illinois. Thomas Jefferson planted pecans at Monticello and sent some to George Washington, who planted them at Mount Vernon. Today these pecans still exist and are the

oldest cultivated plants on the plantation.

Pecans are native as far north as Indiana, Illinois, and Iowa and as far south as Mexico.

COMMON NAME: *Holly, American*

BOTANICAL NAME: *Ilex opaca*

FAMILY: Aquifoliaceae (Holly)

DESCRIPTION: American holly can grow up to 50 feet tall. The evergreen leaves are leathery, dark green on top, pale green underneath. The leaf edges are marked by spiny teeth. *I. latifolia*, lusterleaf holly, grows to about 40 feet tall and has attractive, shiny leaves. Some of the most popular cultivars, such as 'Nellie Stevens', are in this genus. This cultivar is of particular importance because it has been bred to produce fruit without a male plant. Holly berries are bright red and are wonderfully attractive in late fall and early winter.

ORIGIN: American holly is native to North America from Massachusetts to Florida, west to Missouri and Texas.

HOW TO GROW: Hollies need full sun or partial shade and moist, well-drained soil. They are often used in hedges or borders and sometimes as specimen plants. American holly tolerates salt air and prefers slightly acidic soil. Grows in zones 5 to 9.

Much superstition and folklore surrounds holly. For example, it was believed that holly flowers could turn water to ice and that holly bushes planted near buildings would serve as protection against lightning and witchcraft.

An ancient legend suggests that holly first began to grow in the footsteps of Jesus Christ. The sharp leaves represent the crown of thorns, and the red berries symbolize blood spilled on the Cross.

Folk healers made tea from the leaves to induce sweating to break a fever. Native Americans in the southern United States used the

highly toxic American holly berries to make a drink used in ritualistic ceremonies. The botanical name *I. vomitoria* gives an indication of what happens when one drinks this concoction. Raw berries are very toxic and cause vomiting and purging.

English holly, *I. aquifolium,* has been used in winter celebrations since the days of the Roman Saturnalia, a festival that began on December 17.

According to the English language of flowers, holly means foresight.

American holly is the state tree of Delaware.

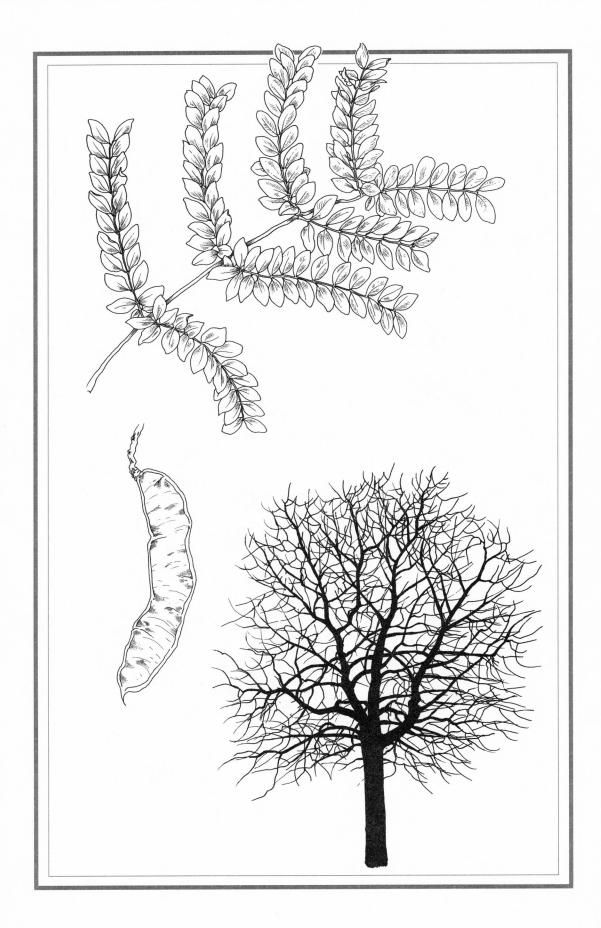

COMMON NAME: *Honey Locust*
BOTANICAL NAME: *Gleditsia triacanthos*
FAMILY: Leguminosae (Pea)

DESCRIPTION: The species *triacanthos* is infamous for its dangerously sharp, pointed thorns. Luckily the variety 'inermis' has been developed, which is both thornless and fruitless. The leaves are compound (sometimes double) and measure 6 to 8 inches long. Twenty to thirty small leaflets on each leaf give the honey locust a feathery appearance. The leaves make a short show as they are late to appear in spring and drop early in fall. In fall the leaves turn a muted yellow color. The bark is dark brown and furrowed. Fragrant greenish white flowers appear in clusters in May. The fruit is a pod, which often spirals before dropping in autumn. Several cultivars are available including 'Shademaster', 'Skyline', and 'Sunburst'.

ORIGIN: Nova Scotia west to South Dakota, south to Oklahoma and Texas, east to Florida

HOW TO GROW: Honey locust likes alkaline soil and full sun. It tolerates many harsh environmental conditions, including salting from highways, air pollution, flooding, and wind damage. It is particularly useful in the garden because it allows dappled sunlight to filter through, making it possible to grow grass or ground covers underneath. Grows in zones 4 to 9.

The long, thin spines from honey locust were used as pins to fasten the cloaks of soldiers during the Civil War.

The American native black locust, *Robinia pseudoacacia,* looks very much like the honey locust. It has very hard, durable wood. Locust posts set into the ground will last fifty years or more.

Seeds of black locust were sent to Jean Robin, botanist to the king of France in the early seventeenth century. The genus *Robinia* was named after him.

The pulp of the pods is very sweet and is readily eaten by both wildlife and livestock.

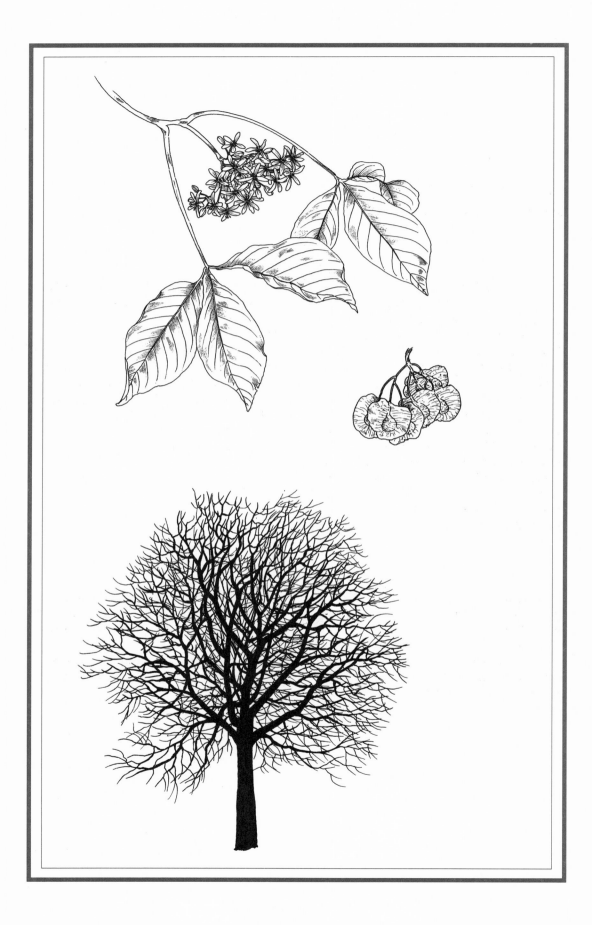

COMMON NAME: *Hoptree*

BOTANICAL NAME: *Ptelea trifoliata*

FAMILY: Rutaceae (Rue)

DESCRIPTION: Hoptree is an open, rounded small tree, growing to a height of about 20 feet. The bark, foliage, and twigs, when crushed, have a highly aromatic but slightly unpleasant odor. The leaves are wide, with a long pointed tip and small gland dots. They are shiny dark green on top, slightly hairy underneath. Several cultivars have been developed from the original species. 'Aurea' has bright yellow leaves; the subspecies 'pallida' has white bark.

ORIGIN: Hoptree is native from southern Ontario east to New York and New Jersey, south to Florida, and west to Texas. Local populations can be found in Arizona and southern Utah.

HOW TO GROW: In nature hoptree is found on dry, rocky slopes and in canyons and valleys. Well-drained soil is an important factor in cultivating hoptree.

Hoptree is a member of the rue, or citrus, family and grows farther north than any other members of this family. It is also known as wafer ash.

The bitter fruit of hoptree one time served as a substitute for hops in brewing beer, thus the common name. The bark of the roots was used extensively in folk medicines. Its reputation as a powerful general tonic was surpassed only by that of goldenseal. Extracts from the plant were often used to strengthen or intensify the effects of other medicines in treating asthma, fever, and digestive disorders.

COMMON NAME: *Juniper*

BOTANICAL NAME: *Juniperus communis*

FAMILY: Cupressaceae (Cypress)

DESCRIPTION: Junipers come in a tremendous variety of shapes and forms. Common juniper, *J. communis*, has foliage that is grouped in three needlelike leaves. It grows 5 to 10 feet tall and spreads 8 to 12 feet wide. *J. virginiana* is also known as eastern red cedar. This species grows to be about 75 feet tall and has deep green scalelike foliage. Several cultivars have been developed from this species, varying in height and form. *J. chinensis* has attractive evergreen foliage and is often used as a ground cover.

ORIGIN: Common juniper has a widespread natural distribution and is native to North America and Eurasia.

HOW TO GROW: Almost all species and varieties can be grown in full sun in acidic to neutral soil. Although the soil can be of average fertility, good drainage is essential. Prune low-growing varieties in spring to stimulate new growth.

Junipers hold many surprising treasures. For example, the blue-black aromatic berries from the common juniper have been used to flavor gin in a process that has been popular for hundreds of years. Although making gin may be the most popular use of juniper, other culinary uses include flavoring game (venison, hare, and goose); making stuffings, soups, and stews; and creating imaginative marinades.

The strongly flavored berries, which must be used sparingly, are good in making pâtés, salads, and even sauerkraut. *Rodale's Illustrated Encyclopedia of Herbs* suggests substituting three or four berries for every bay leaf called for in a recipe. Other parts of juniper can also be used for flavoring. Small branches of the tree or shrub placed over a cooking grill give food a slightly smoky flavor.

A word of caution: Not everyone can tolerate juniper in food. It has been found that large quantities can be mildly toxic to some people. Pregnant women and people with kidney trouble should avoid using it even in small quantities.

In past centuries magical powers were attributed to junipers. They were once planted at the entrance to a home because they allegedly kept away witches. It was thought that a witch could pass a juniper tree only when she had correctly counted all the needles on the tree.

Juniper plants are either male or female, and berries are borne only on the female plant. If junipers are grown primarily for their berries, both male and female plants should be planted.

COMMON NAME: *Kentucky Coffee Tree*

BOTANICAL NAME: *Gymnocladus dioica*

FAMILY: Leguminosae (Pea)

DESCRIPTION: The leaves are twice compound, giving it a feathery look. There are generally three to seven pairs of leaflets. The entire leaf measures about 36 inches long. The tree grows to a height of 75 to 80 feet and spreads almost 40 feet across. The dark gray or black bark is scaly and ridged. The branches create a free-flowing pattern, which give the tree an interesting silhouette during winter months. The greenish white flowers are small and inconspicuous. The fruit is a pod about 5 to 10 inches long.

ORIGIN: Kentucky coffee tree is native to New York and Pennsylvania, west to Nebraska and Oklahoma, and south to Tennessee

HOW TO GROW: Kentucky coffee tree needs full sun or partial shade. Although it tolerates city pollution, it grows best if given fertile soil. The pods are found only on female trees and are sometimes considered a nuisance. Male trees are often planted along city streets. Grows in zones 4 to 8.

Kentucky coffee tree was one of the first trees sent back to Europe from the New World. Other names for this tree include chicot or dead tree because the leaves drop so early in fall. Kentucky mahogany, mahogany bean, and stump tree are additional common names.

Heavy-grained and coarse, the wood of the Kentucky coffee tree is not particularly desirable. It is durable and is sometimes used for railroad ties and fence posts. It was not used extensively even for this purpose, however, because the tree characteristically forks close to the ground.

The pulp from the wood, which is a caramel color, was used by the American Indians to treat insanity. Tea made from the leaves and pulp was taken as a laxative. Tea made from the root bark was made into a cough medicine and was given to women in childbirth.

Many parts of this tree are considered toxic.

The large seeds were ground and used as a coffee substitute, probably based on the way they looked rather than the way they tasted. The pods were of great value to the American Indians.

There is only one close relative of the Kentucky coffee tree, *G. chinense*, or the Chinese soap tree. The seeds of this species have a soap-like quality.

COMMON NAME: *Laurel*

BOTANICAL NAME: *Laurus nobilis*

FAMILY: Lauraceae (Laurel)

DESCRIPTION: Laurel is an evergreen shrub that grows to a height of 10 to 12 feet. The lance-shaped, 4-inch-long leaves are dull dark green and leathery. They emit a lovely fragrance. The blossoms are small, white, and inconspicuous. They appear in spring and are followed by ½-inch blue-black berries.

ORIGIN: Mediterranean region

HOW TO GROW: Bay laurel needs full sun or partial shade and rich, well-drained soil. Give it generous amounts of water during spring but leave on the dry side the remainder of the year. Plant in spring or fall and prune in summer to maintain a nice shape. The shrubs grow slowly. Grows in zones 8 to 10.

Laurel, bay laurel, or sweet bay are all names for the ancient plant *Laurus nobilis,* or the noble or renowned laurel, symbolic of glory. The ancient Romans cooked with it, bathed in it, and crowned their heroes with wreaths made from its branches.

The legend of the origin of laurel is found in a Greek myth. Apollo, god of the sun, fell in love with the beautiful nymph Daphne. Cupid, however, shot a wicked arrow that hit Daphne, causing her to hate Apollo. Apollo continued to pursue Daphne until finally, in desperation, Daphne's father, Peneus, turned Daphne into a laurel tree. Apollo fell to his knees before this tree and swore that it would be eternally sacred. From that time on he wore a wreath of laurel leaves on his head in memory of Daphne. *Daphne* is the Greek name for laurel. (For a slightly different version of this myth, see Daphne, page 73.)

Laurel leaves woven into victors' crowns were worn by both Romans and Greeks. Athletes, kings, poets, and priests all proudly wore laurel crowns.

Because the tree was held in such great esteem, whenever it died it was considered an ill omen by the ancient Greeks and Romans.

Laurel was thought to have uncommonly strong powers of protection. In 1575 Thomas Lupton wrote that "neyther falling sickness, neyther deveyll, wyll infest or hurt one in that place where a bay tree is." In addition it was thought that a bay laurel tree could provide safety from lightning.

Laurel has been used for a multitude of purposes for many centuries. Medicinally bay laurel has been used to treat stomachaches and rheumatism and has served as an astringent and a stimulant.

In the kitchen bay laurel is used extensively in tomato sauces, soups, and stews, as well as in the preparation of shellfish and game.

COMMON NAME: *Lilac*

BOTANICAL NAME: *Syringa vulgaris*

FAMILY: Oleaceae (Olive)

DESCRIPTION: Lilacs put on a spectacular display of fragrant blossoms in spring. Individual flowers have four petals and are clustered together in a spike. Flower colors come in all shades of mauves and purples, with light purple, or lilac, being the most common color. Many cultivars and varieties have been developed to extend the blooming season or to add slightly different flower colors. Lilacs are generally rather ordinary looking when not in bloom, but the unforgettable fragrance and beauty of the blossoms make them well worth growing. *S. vulgaris* grows about 20 feet tall.

ORIGIN: The common lilac is native to southeastern Europe.

HOW TO GROW: Lilacs do not tolerate hot, humid conditions. They prefer full sun but tolerate some shade. Rich, moist, well-drained soil is best. They grow in zones 3 to 7.

The word *lilac* is an Old English word that has its roots in the Arabic word *laylak* and the Perisan word *nilak,* from *nil* meaning "blue." The genus name *syringa* means "tube" in Greek, which refers to the configuration of each individual flower.

So important are lilacs to New Englanders that lilac-blooming season is called the "lilac tide." It is believed that lilacs were first brought to this country in the late seventeenth century. One story often told is that Sir Harry Frankland, an Englishman of great wealth, had a mistress living in New England. Knowing of her love of flowers, he gave her many unusual and exotic plants, including a lilac bush.

A different story suggests that the first American lilacs were brought here from Persia by an English sea captain. George Washington was known to have grown lilacs at Mount Vernon when he retired there to devote his time to horticultural ventures, and Jefferson wrote in his diary on April 2, 1729, that he also planted lilacs.

Lilacs played both a symbolic and horticultural role in Colonial Williamsburg. It became customary to place a bowl of white lilacs before the portrait of Catherine of Braganza, the queen of Charles II of England.

Pioneers carving a home in the wilderness of the American West bought lilacs from plant peddlers and planted them close to their doorsteps—a lovely and fragrant reminder of the homes that they had left in the East.

In the West Indies lilacs bloomed prolifically and soon became a symbol of peace and prosperity.

Perhaps the world's largest lilac collection is at Harvard's Arnold Arboretum. More than 500 varieties of the common lilac are grown there, as well as French, Persian, white, and tree lilacs.

The first emotions of love are symbolized by purple lilac blossoms, while white lilac flowers signify purity, modesty, and youth.

Lilac is the state flower of New Hampshire.

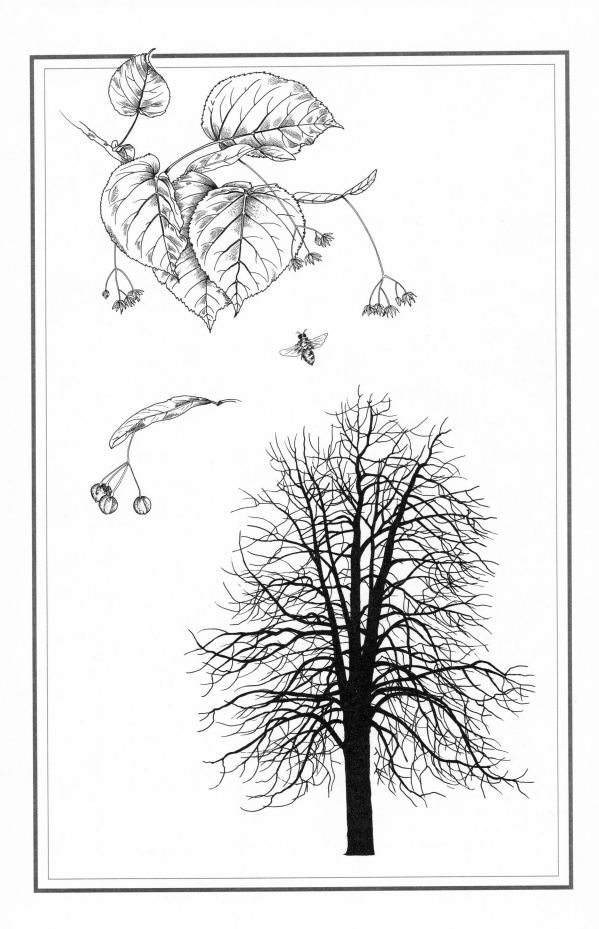

COMMON NAME: *Linden*

BOTANICAL NAME: *Tilia americana*

FAMILY: Tiliaceae (Linden)

DESCRIPTION: American linden grows 50 to 80 feet tall and has a narrow crown. The leaves are alternate, toothed and heart-shaped, about 4 to 8 inches long. The small, fragrant yellow flowers appear in summer. Leaves turn a butternut yellow in fall. Other species include *T. cordata*, the little-leaf linden, and *T. tomentosa*, silver linden, which has silvery white on the undersides of the leaves.

ORIGIN: Eurasia

HOW TO GROW: Lindens need full sun and moist, well-drained soil. During dormancy, the trees are easily transplanted. Linden makes a good shade tree, as it grows quickly. Grows in zones 5 to 8.

The Linden tree has a multitude of common names including basswood, bee-tree, black lime-tree, lime tree, linn, whitewood, and wickup.

American Indians made a tea from the inner bark to treat lung disorders and upset stomachs. Folk medicine called for using the buds, leaves, and flowers to alleviate headaches and insomnia. Scientists warn that protracted use of tea made from the flowers may be harmful, causing damage to the heart.

The heartwood is creamy white to brown, sometimes even leaning toward red. The lightweight wood averages 26 pounds per cubic foot. Unfortunately the wood is relatively weak and shrinks a great deal while drying. The lumber is used for general purposes such as crates and boxes and core materials for making panels.

COMMON NAME: *Magnolia, Southern*

BOTANICAL NAME: *Magnolia grandiflora*

FAMILY: Magnoliaceae (Magnolia)

DESCRIPTION: The stately magnolia tree is a large evergreen, growing as much as 80 feet tall. It spreads about 40 feet across and has graceful low branching. The young branches are rusty brown, as are the undersides of the leaves. The large, leathery leaves, measuring 6 inches long, are shiny green on top. The creamy white blossoms usually have six petals (sometimes nine or twelve) and are highly fragrant. The fruit is a heavy, long pod, exposing bright red seeds in fall. Other species, cultivars, and varieties are of equal ornamental value. *M. acuminata*, cucumber tree, is a deciduous tree growing 50 to 80 feet tall, which produces 3-inch-long cup-shaped yellowish green flowers. *M.* x soulangiana, saucer magnolia, is a small deciduous tree, 20 to 30 feet tall with bright pink or purple blossoms, which are surprisingly white on the inside. The bark is smooth and light gray.

ORIGIN: North Carolina to Florida, west to Texas

HOW TO GROW: Magnolias should be planted from balled or container-grown plants in spring in soil that is deep, well-drained, rich in organic matter, and slightly acidic. Watering and mulching during dry periods will greatly benefit the trees. Once they have been planted, do not disturb the root system even by planting bulbs. Grows in zones 7 to 9.

The great flowered magnolia is the state flower of Mississippi and Louisiana. It was named for Pierre Magnol (1638–1715), who was director of the botanical garden at Montpellier, France.

Magnolia is also known as bat tree, big laurel, bullbay, laurel, and sweet magnolia. Magnolias are very ancient trees. Fossil records show that they grew long before the arrival of modern man.

The Chinese were the first to cultivate magnolias. The trees were first grown for utilitarian rather than for ornamental purposes. The Chinese used the buds to flavor rice and medicines.

Tea made from the bark of cucumber magnolia was substituted for quinine to treat malaria or typhoid. The bark was sometimes chewed as an aid in smoking cessation.

A wonderful specimen of magnolia grows outside the White House. It was planted by Andrew Jackson in honor of his wife, Rachel.

Magnolia wood is used for cabinetwork, for veneer, and for making boxes and crates.

Asian species of this tree are considered an emblem of purity. According to the English language of flowers, magnolia is symbolic of a love of nature.

COMMON NAME: *Maple*

BOTANICAL NAME: *Acer* sp.

FAMILY: Aceraceae (Maple)

DESCRIPTION: Maples grow in height from 15 to 100 feet. The leaves are either simple and lobed or compound and opposite. The flowers are unisexual and occur in panicles in early spring. Red maples, *A. rubrum*, have leaves 2 to 4 inches long with three to five lobes. In fall the foliage is yellow or bright red. Red spring flowers appear before the leaves emerge. Sugar maple, *A. saccharum*, grows to 100 feet. The leaves are 4 to 6 inches long and have three to five lobes. Light yellow spring flowers are inconspicuous, but the foliage in fall turns a beautiful orangey red or yellow. Silver maple, *A. saccharinum*, grows to 100 feet. It has gray bark and deeply lobed leaves, light green on top and silvery white underneath. The flowers have no petals and come out very early in spring.

ORIGIN: Maples grow in north-temperate zones. There are about 150 species in the genus, *Acer*, varying in size and shape. Red maples are found in the east from Newfoundland to Florida and west to Texas and Minnesota. Sugar maple grows only as far south as Georgia. Silver maple grows as far west as Oklahoma.

HOW TO GROW: Maples are very desirable as ornamental and shade trees. Sugar maples need good, rich soil and have several outstanding cultivars including 'Bonfire', named for its brilliant autumn foliage, and 'Green Mountain', with attractive dark green leaves. Silver maple is a fast-growing tree with fragile, brittle twigs and branches, easily broken by storms and high winds. Red maple is slightly smaller (up to 70 feet) and is often used as a shade tree. It tolerates a wide range of cultural conditions.

Sugar maples provided sugar for pioneer families, and maple syrup is still highly prized. The quality of the syrup depends on the soil and climate of the region. Pioneer families used hollow elder and sumac branches to put into the maple trees to collect the sap, which dripped into buckets attached to the trees. These branches were later replaced by metal pipes. Today plastic tubing goes directly from the heartwood of the trees to sugar camps, where the sap is boiled down to syrup. A single tree can give as much as 5 to 60 gallons of sap a year. It takes approximately 32 gallons of sap to make a gallon of syrup.

Canyon maple, the western counterpart to the eastern sugar maple, has a sweet sap often used to make syrup. The wood of canyon maple is heavy, hard, and close grained. The heartwood is very light brown, the sapwood thick and white. The wood is much sought after for firewood, and the leaves turn brilliant colors in autumn.

New Englanders often drank spoonfuls of the sap straight as a spring tonic. The syrup was considered good for liver and kidney problems and was also sometimes used in cough syrups. American Indians treated coughs and diarrhea with tea made from the inner bark. Maple bark was sometimes used by early pioneers as dye.

Striped maple, *A. pensylvanicum*, so named because of its gray-and-white-striped bark, has several interesting common names. It is called goosefoot maple because the leaves are thought to look somewhat like the webbed foot of a gander. It is also called whistlewood because the bark peels off easily, making the creation of whistles much easier, and it is called moosewood because moose like to eat the young stalks.

A maple blossom was thought to signify "reserve," according to the Victorian language of flowers.

Red maple is the state tree of Rhode Island. Sugar maple is the state tree of New York, Vermont, West Virginia, and Wisconsin.

COMMON NAME: *Mesquite*

BOTANICAL NAME: *Prosopis glandulosa*

FAMILY: Leguminosae (Pea)

DESCRIPTION: Mesquite grows about 30 feet tall and often spreads an equal distance. Small branches and twigs of this species have long, sharp thorns. The twice-compound leaves have one or two pairs of branchlets, each one having six to twenty pairs of bright green leaflets. Yellowish green small flowers appear in late spring and summer.

ORIGIN: southern California to Arizona, Texas, and Mexico

HOW TO GROW: Mesquite is extremely useful as a desert shade tree in the Southwest. It is also used as a windbreak or screen. Although it is tolerant of drought conditions when mature, young trees need ample moisture. Without sufficient moisture, the plants will not grow to be tree size.

Mesquite today is found within a wide range, but it grows so rapidly that it is considered a pesky weed in grasslands. The name mesquite is derived from the Aztec name *mizquitl*.

The extension of its range can be traced directly back to the days of cattle drives. Cattle ate the pods of the mesquite in its natural range, near the Texas-Mexico border. As the cattle were driven north toward market, the seeds passed through the cows and were then deposited on new land in cow patties. The seeds germinated and grew, producing plants and seeds that, in turn, were eaten by the next drove of cattle

coming through the area, and so on until mesquite finally spread throughout Oklahoma, Kansas, and southeastern Colorado.

Screwbean mesquite is a closely related species. Humans as well as livestock and wildlife enjoy eating the sweet and tasty pods of this species. American Indians ate the pods and sometimes made them into syrup. The pods were even made into a flavorful alcoholic drink.

The seed pods were so valuable as horse fodder that the United States Cavalry paid 3 cents a pound for mesquite beans for their horses when traveling through New Mexico. Laboratory

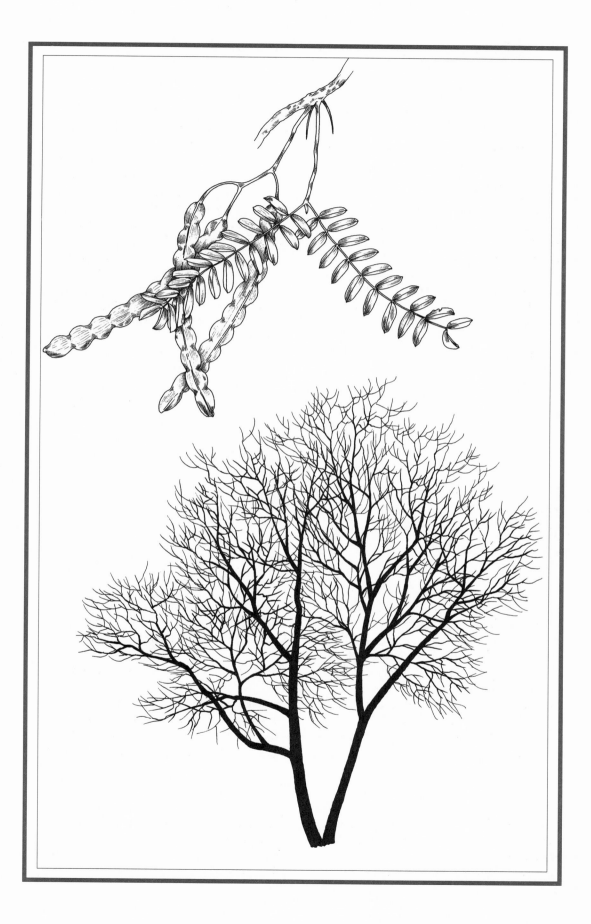

tests found that the pods contain 25 to 30 percent sugar and are greatly enjoyed by livestock.

The root bark was sometimes made into a poultice to treat skin disorders.

Mesquite has two distinct blooming seasons. The first occurs after the winter rains in April, the second in June and July, when blooming continues intermittently until fall. Bees swarm to mesquite trees when they are in bloom, creating a honey that is a clear amber color.

Southwestern Indians used mesquite wood for many purposes. They played a variety of kickball with a hard ball made from mesquite and shaped pottery with mesquite paddles. They even made plows from the sharpened wood.

Gum from the tree was chewed by the Indi-

ans and was used to repair pottery and also to treat wounds and sores. In 1871 12,000 pounds of gum were gathered in a single county in Texas and sent to the East Coast to make gumdrops.

The bark was used in tanning and dyeing.

Some individual mesquite trees have gained far-reaching fame. The "jail tree," found in Wickenburg, Arizona, was a detaining place for criminals in days past. The "badmen" were roped or chained to the tree until their sentence was served. A giant mesquite, with a trunk nearly 15 feet in circumference, was found on the grounds of the Santa Cruz Valley School in Tumacacori, Arizona. The schoolchildren affectionately named it "Old Geronimo."

COMMON NAME: *Mimosa*

BOTANICAL NAME: *Albizia julibrissin*

FAMILY: Leguminosae (Pea)

DESCRIPTION: Mimosa is a delicate-looking tree growing to a height of about 40 feet. The branches are low and wide spreading. The leaves are 9 to 12 inches long and are divided into fourteen to twenty finely dissected leaflets, which resemble fern fronds. The fragrant flowers look like bright pink powder puffs. The fruits are long pods that look like pea pods. Cultivars 'Charlotte' and 'Tryon' are resistant to mimosa wilt disease.

ORIGIN: Mimosa is native from Iran to Japan but is now naturalized from Maryland and Indiana south to Florida and Louisiana.

HOW TO GROW: Mimosa trees like full sun and well-drained soil. They are tolerant of dry soils and urban pollution. They are susceptible to a disease known as mimosa wilt disease, which eventually kills the trees. Resistant cultivars are recommended. Grows in zones 6 to 9.

The name mimosa was given to this tree because of its resemblance to the sensitive plants of the genus *Mimosa*. While the leaves of true mimosa fold up when touched, the leaves of the mimosa

tree sometimes fold at night in order to reduce surface area when the temperature drops.

Mimosa is also known as silktree because of the soft and silken flowers that cover the tree in

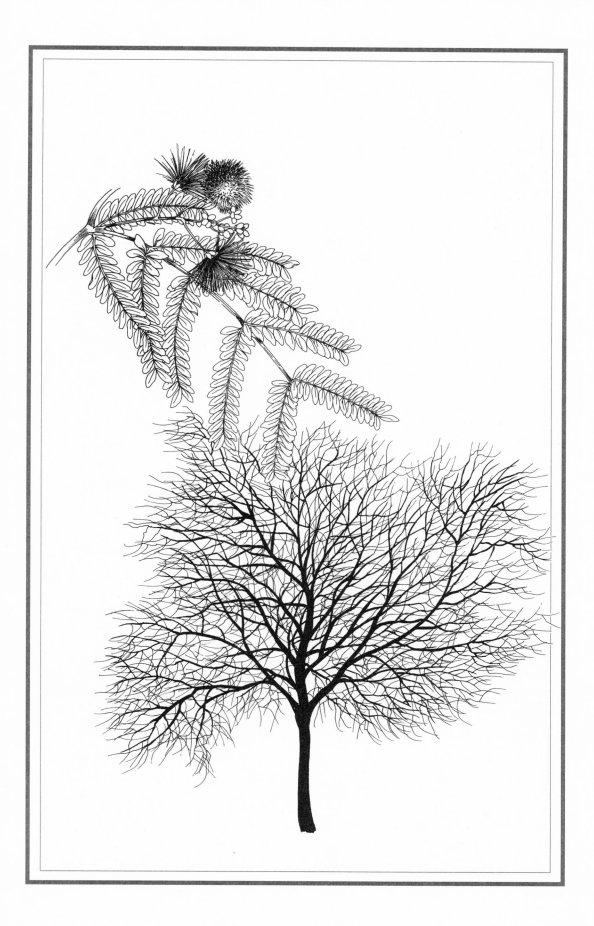

spring. Although the tree has no real economic value for its lumber and only limited value as an ornamental tree, its worth to little girls playing dress-up in the early days of summer is unsurpassed. The flowers make ideal powderpuffs. They are soft, fragrant, and decidedly feminine.

Mimosa trees have been cultivated in China since ancient times. The tree was introduced to Europe in 1745 and is named for Filippo del Albizzia, an eighteenth-century naturalist.

A related species, *A. lebbek*, has long, flat tan seedpods that hang down and persist for several months. When dry, the seedpods rattle and chatter with every passing breeze, giving rise to the nickname, "woman's tongue." In spite of this, according to the English language of flowers, mimosa is the symbol for courtesy.

COMMON NAME: *Monkey Pine*

BOTANICAL NAME: *Araucaria araucana*

FAMILY: Araucariaceae (Araucaria)

DESCRIPTION: Monkey pine, or monkey puzzle tree, grows to 90 feet and has open, rope-like branches with very sharp needles. The bark is gray with rings. The tree is evergreen and grows in a pyramid shape. *A. heterophylla*, Norfolk Island pine (also known as Australian house pine), is in the same genus. It is a popular subtropical species commonly grown as a houseplant. In its natural state Norfolk Island pine grows 70 feet or more.

ORIGIN: *A. araucana* is native to Chile. *A. heterophylla* is native to Norfolk Island, Australia.

HOW TO GROW: Monkey pine can be used alone as a specimen tree or in groups to create a windbreak. The cones are large and heavy, however, and can be somewhat dangerous. It does best grown in full sun and moist soils. It grows in zones 8 and 9. Norfolk Island pine needs partial shade but tolerates a wide range of conditions. It can be grown outdoors during the warm months but should be brought indoors when the weather turns cool. It is hardy outdoors only in zone 10.

Monkey pine is also known as Chilean pine or monkey puzzle. It is indigenous to a small area of southwest Argentina and a section of Chile. It was first found growing in the province of Arauco, thus the genus name.

The wood of monkey pine is yellowish gray in color and darkens as it ages. It has straight grains and a fine texture. Because the wood dries so unevenly and is so long in drying, it must be cured carefully.

Wood from Chilean pine has been exported to Great Britian for more than 150 years. Primarily used for interior woodwork such as doors and window ledges, it is also used in airplane con-

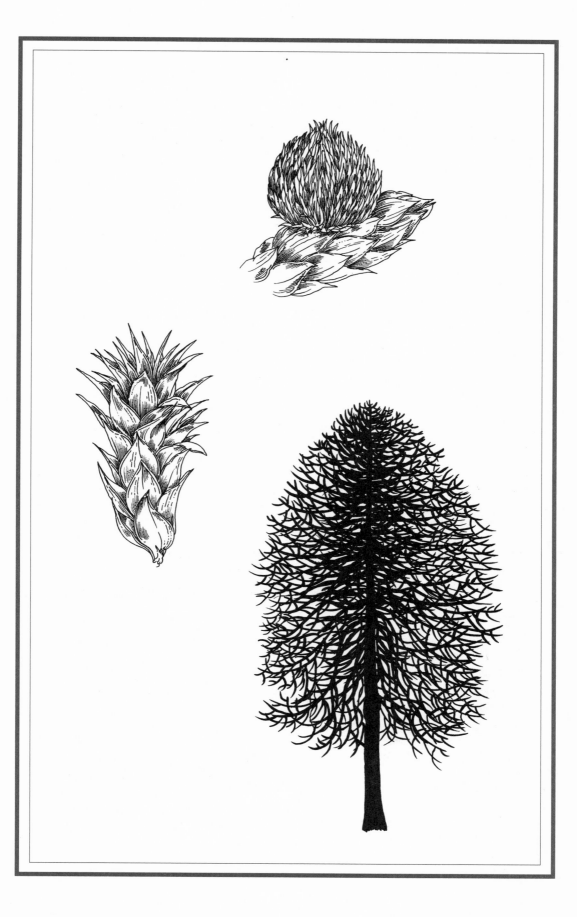

struction. Because the trees grow in the wild so high up in mountainous regions and is therefore difficult to get to, very little wood is exported today.

The seeds occur in huge quantities, often numbering more than one hundred per cone. Native Chileans gathered these and roasted them, considering them a rare delicacy.

COMMON NAME: *Mountain Laurel*

BOTANICAL NAME: *Kalmia latifolia*

FAMILY: Ericaceae (Heath)

DESCRIPTION: Mountain laurel is an evergreen shrub, sometimes considered a small tree. It generally reaches a height of 20 feet. The trunk is stout and crooked with spreading branches. The attractive flowers are cup-shaped and occur in clusters. Petals may be pink, white, or rose, and long brown stamens give the flowers a speckled look. The leaves are dark green, shiny, and leathery. The bark is reddish brown and peeling, and the inner bark is dark. One of the best cultivars is 'Clementine Churchill', which has deep red flowers, as does the variety Ostobo Red.

ORIGIN: Mountain laurel is native from Maine south to northern Florida and west to Louisiana.

HOW TO GROW: Mountain laurel grows naturally in the understory of a mixed forest. In the home landscape the shrubs need full sun or partial shade and rich, moist, acidic soil. Pruning after the plant blooms helps to maintain an attractive appearance throughout the year. Because the roots are shallow, they benefit from a deep cover of mulch during cold or dry periods. It is hardy to zone 5.

The stamens of mountain laurel have a spring-like mechanism that releases pollen to the air when tripped by bees. The leaves are poisonous to livestock, and honey made from the blossoms is also considered poisonous. Deer and ruffed grouse feed on the foliage, buds, and twigs. The shrub offers a good source of shelter for wildlife throughout the year.

Although the plant is highly toxic, there have been limited medicinal uses for mountain laurel. American Indians applied a poultice made from the bark and leaves to soothe pain from rheumatism, and it was occasionally included in insecticidal soaps.

Mountain laurel tea was taken internally with great risk. Tiny amounts of it were drunk to treat syphilis and heart diseases. Because the plant is so high in toxins, however, taking it internally is highly discouraged.

According to the language of flowers, mountain laurel is a symbol of ambition.

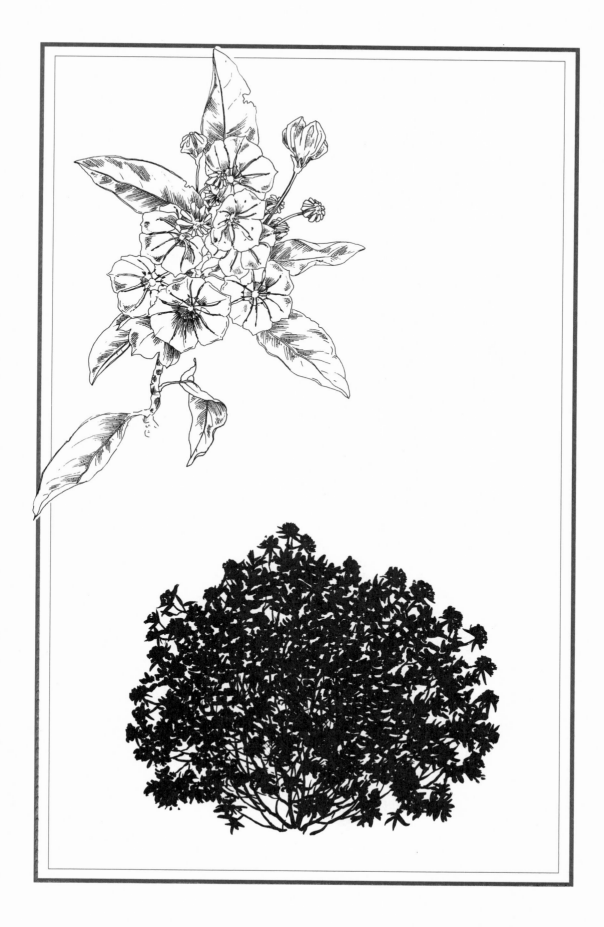

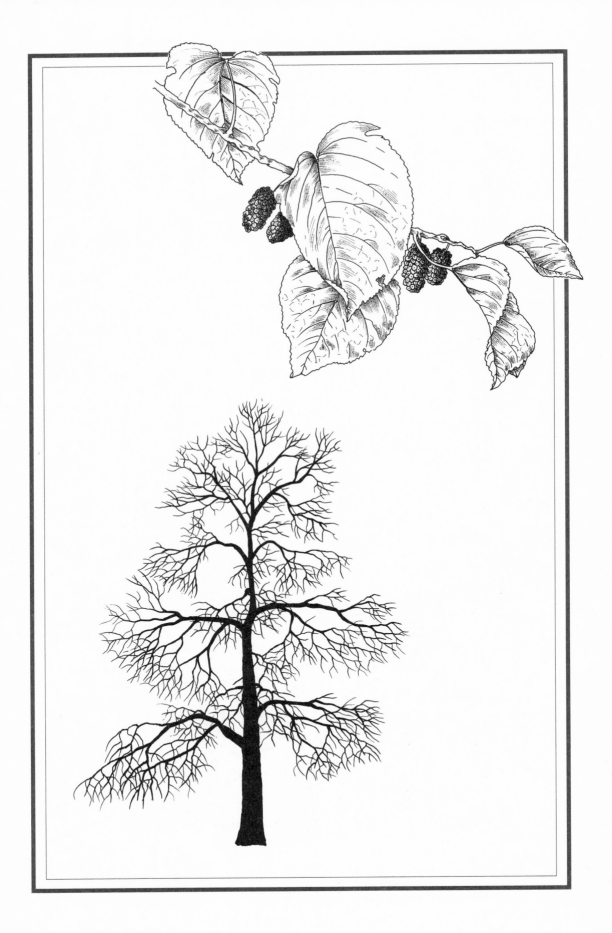

COMMON NAME: *Mulberry, White*
BOTANICAL NAME: *Morus alba*
FAMILY: Moraceae (Mulberry)

DESCRIPTION: Although the species tree has fruit that many consider messy in the garden, several nonfruiting cultivars have been developed. Among the best are 'Kingan', 'Fruitless', and 'Stribling'. Cultivars grow 35 to 40 feet tall and are rounded on top. The alternate leaves are toothed and sometimes lobed, and they show little fall color.

ORIGIN: China

HOW TO GROW: Mulberry needs full sun or partial shade and rich, well-drained soil, although it is tolerant of a wide range of soil types. The species tree makes a good specimen tree, and the fruitless varieties are useful as shade trees. It needs annual pruning to maintain a nice shape. Grows in zones 5 to 9.

White mulberry is also known as silkworm mulberry or Russian mulberry. For many centuries it has been cultivated as the main food source for silkworms. When settlers moved to the southeastern United States, many of them introduced mulberries in great quantities in an attempt to produce silk. Unfortunately, the silk industry never became profitable in the region, and soon the venture was abandoned.

Mulberries grow rapidly and produce a multitude of seeds, which are consumed by many kinds of birds. Cultivars include a weeping form and a fruitless form.

Many parts of the white mulberry tree were used medicinally. Tea made from the leaves alleviated headaches and soothed coughs. Tea made from the young twigs eased pain in the joints. The fruit was thought to be helpful to diabetics and was also eaten to improve blood circulation and strengthen the blood. Tea made from the inner bark of the tree was used to treat respiratory ailments.

Black mulberry weighs about 40 pounds per cubic foot. Its bright yellow color becomes a rich gold when aged. The grain is very attractive and is much valued for chair work.

Southwestern Indians cultivated the white mulberry tree. A small grove can still be found in a side canyon of the Grand Canyon where Havasupai Indians grew them.

COMMON NAME: *Oak*

BOTANICAL NAME: *Quercus* sp.

FAMILY: Fagaceae (Beech)

DESCRIPTION: The *Quercus* genus comprises 450 different species. They range in mature height from 35 to 100 feet and are found throughout the United States from tropical regions to cold northern zones. Many species are evergreen. Leaves may be lobed, entire, or divided. Both male and female flowers are borne on the same tree and produce fruit, called an acorn. *Q. alba,* white oak, grows 100 feet tall. It is slow growing and rounded at the top. The leaves have five to nine lobes and turn dark brownish purple in fall. Origin: eastern North America. Grows in zones 4 to 9. *Q. palustris,* pin oak, forms a broad pyramidal shape and grows 75 to 80 feet tall. The leaves have five to nine deep lobes and are bright green, changing to bronze or deep red in autumn. Origin: eastern North America. Grows in zones 5 to 9. *Q. virginiana,* live oak, is evergreen, usually not growing over 75 to 80 feet in height and spreading 60 to 100 feet. The branches are gnarled and interesting, the leaves 3 to 5 inches long and oblong. Live oak cannot tolerate temperatures below

zero. Origin: Virginia to Florida and Mexico. Grows in zones 7 to 10. *Q. gambelii,* gambel oak, is most closely related to the eastern white oak. It grows abundantly in the Rocky Mountains and in the Grand Canyon National Park. Different kinds of wildlife, including wild turkeys and squirrels, feed on the acorns of this species. It is named for a naturalist from Philadelphia, William Gambel (1821–1849). *Q. garryana,* Oregon white oak, has the greatest commercial value of any of the western oaks. The wood is used in the shipbuilding and construction industries and for making furniture and providing fuel. The acorns are sweet in comparison to the fruit from other oaks but are abundant only in alternate years.

ORIGIN: See Description.

HOW TO GROW: Many oaks actually prefer growing in heavy, clay soils but, as a general rule, like deep, rich acidic soil. They all like full sun.

Members of the white-oak group have been used extensively for making utensils for holding liquids. Missouri Ozark white oaks are made into barrels that supply distilleries throughout the world. Coopers, or barrel makers, cut the wood so that the ray tissues in the wood stop the flow of liquids. Without cutting it in this special way, alcohol would seep through. Staves, headings, and hoops are also made from white oak.

Chestnut oak, sometimes called tanbark oak, provides the leather industry with tannic acid,

which is extracted from the bark. Tannic acid helps to preserve and dye hides as well as protect them from mildew and rot.

Oak heartwood is extremely hard and makes solid fence posts and rails. White oak wood is sometimes quarter-sawed, which creates "mirrors" prized by cabinetmakers; that is, the wood is cut so light is reflected on it to show wood of two colors. The practice of quartersawing was begun in the 1880s. Tough white oak was sometimes used for making durable axles for wagons.

Oregon white oak was used to make buckets, guitars, and handles for tools. Shingles were made from split white oak. Many Native American tribes ate acorns as a food staple and made medicine from the bark. Brewed into a tea, the bark relieved diarrhea. The colonists applied the bark on wounds and open sores as an astringent. Modern research has found that the astringent qualities of oak cause the capillaries of the skin to constrict, making this an effective means of stopping minor bleeding.

A concoction made from white oak was also used as a folk remedy for cancer. A wash made from the inner bark was put on wounds and skin disorders. Like many folk cancer cures, substances in white oak may be toxic.

Cork oak, *Q. suber*, grows in the Mediterranean region. When the trees are about thirty years old, workers strip away the bark and make lightweight bottle stoppers. Restripping on trees

is done every ten years, sometimes for centuries. Most cork comes from Spain, Portugal, and Morocco; some comes from California.

Red oak trees are not used for cooperage because the pores are not filled with gum as they are in the white oak group. But for this reason, red oak wood takes preservatives better, making it desirable for railroad crossties and mine props.

White oak was called "Jove's own tree" and was sometimes worshiped. Shakespeare wrote of "oak cleaving thunderbolts" in *King Lear*.

In English history, common folks were taxed according to how many swine their oak forest could support with its acorn crop.

Northern red oak is the state tree of New Jersey. White oak is the state tree of Connecticut and of Maryland; native oak, of Illinois, and live oak, of Georgia.

COMMON NAME: *Olive*

BOTANICAL NAME: *Olea europaea*

FAMILY: Oleaceae (Olive)

DESCRIPTION: Olive trees grow about 30 feet tall and have gnarled, ridged stems. The silvery gray-green leaves are 1 to 3 inches long. The flowers are small and white, borne in panicles. The fruit is green, changing to purplish black, and is edible.

ORIGIN: Olive trees are native to the hottest parts of the Mediterranean region.

HOW TO GROW: Some experts suggest that if grown in dry, infertile soils, the tree will form a more gnarled and aged look. To maintain a more sedate and "normal" tree appearance, plant in deep, well-drained rich soil and prune annually to remove suckers and lower branches. Although the tree performs well in hot, dry areas, it needs chilling to at least 50 degrees during winter months to flower and fruit. Grows in zones 9 in 10, semihardy in zone 8.

Olive trees can grow to be very old, sometimes living more than 100 years.

The wood is yellow, streaked with dark brown pigment lines. The lumber is most valuable as a veneer, and is expensive. Sometimes burls are available.

Untreated tree-ripened olives are so bitter that they are hardly edible. Extensive processing is necessary to obtain the delicious fruit that we eat today. Generally ripe olives (both green and black) are picked in October. After harvest, the olives are held in brine for several months and are then soaked in a dilute lye solution that helps to get rid of the bitter taste. At this point black olives are differentiated from the green ones. Black olives are aerated, a process that causes the skin and meat to turn dark.

Olives enjoy a rich and varied history. According to the Bible a dove brought an olive branch to Noah indicating that the flood waters had receded.

In a story from Greek mythology, Athena, goddess of peace and war, of the arts, and of wisdom gave the olive to mankind. The olive soon became symbolic of peace and honor, and victorious Olympian athletes were crowned with olive branches.

Olive oil held great economic importance in early days, and a man's wealth was often measured by the amount of olive oil he owned. The oil is still used for many things including food, an important component in the pharmaceutical industry, and soaps and lubricants in the cosmetic industry. Oil obtained from crushing the mature fruit is an important commercial crop.

In the United States olives are grown most often in California. Records indicate that the first olive trees were planted at the mission of San Diego de Alcola in 1769. In 1900 the University of California developed a safe, efficient means of curing olives, thus ensuring California a stable place in the world's olive market.

COMMON NAME: *Palm, Coconut*

BOTANICAL NAME: *Cocos nucifera*

FAMILY: Palmae (Palm)

DESCRIPTION: Coconut palm has a straight trunk and a magnificent tuft of graceful, nodding leaf branches coming from the crown. Each leaf branch is 12 to 18 feet long. The leaves are leathery and evergreen. When the tree is approximately five years old, it starts producing fruit, the familiar coconut. The tree grows to a height of 100 to 130 feet.

ORIGIN: Unknown (probably tropical Melanesia)

HOW TO GROW: Coconut palms are often used to line streets in tropical areas. They have few cultural needs and are tolerant of salt spray and pollution. The trees should be planted in full sun and sandy soils to which organic matter has been added. Grows in zones 8 to 10.

The coconut is considered the most important commercial nut in the world. It is prized for its meat and milk, for charcoal made from the shells, for lumber from the trunk, and for fibers from the husks, which are used to make brushes, cloth, and rope.

The story is told that Florida's first palm trees grew as a result of the shipwreck of the ship *Providencia,* which was carrying thousands of coconuts from the South Seas. The ship went down close to the beach near Lake Worth on January 9, 1878. Consequently, the coconuts floated to shore, took root, and supposedly within ten years the area had 350,000 coconut palm trees.

The coconut palm is thought to be native to the ancient Pacific islands, or perhaps the west coast of South America. The huge seeds were carried from one island to the next until they were eventually cultivated.

According to the English language of flowers, palms are symbols of victory.

Coconut palm is the state tree of Hawaii.

COMMON NAME: *Palm, Date*

BOTANICAL NAME: *Phoenix canariensis*

FAMILY: Palmae (Palm)

DESCRIPTION: At full maturity the date palm attains a height of 50 to 60 feet. The gracefully arching leaves are 15 to 20 feet long. They are evergreen and reach out from the top of a large, stout, straight trunk. At full growth the trunk may be 3 feet in diameter. It takes approximately ten to fifteen years for the tree to bear clusters of red dates. The bark has a diamond-shaped pattern. *Washingtonia robusta,* Mexican fan palm, is commonly grown in California, New Mexico, and Arizona, along the Gulf Coast, and in Florida. It grows about 90 feet tall and has large segmented leaf blades that create a fan effect.

ORIGIN: Date palm is native to the Canary Islands. Mexican fan palm is native to Mexico.

HOW TO GROW: Date palm is often used to line streets or driveways in California and the Canary Islands. It needs full sun and fertile soil. To discourage aphids, it is useful to hose down the leaves periodically. Grows in zones 9 and 10. Mexican fan palm grows in zones 9 and 10.

Palms are among the oldest of all flowering trees. Pollen grains have been found in organic swamp sediments that date back around 10,000 years. Palms exhibit an unusual growth habit.

Because of a lack of conduction tissues common in most other trees, the trees do not grow in circumference as they age. In addition, the number of leaves on the trees stays constant.

Palms are among the tallest trees on earth. A palm species in Colombia measures over 200 feet in height.

In third-world countries where palms are indigenous, many products are derived from these trees. The sap provides an inexpensive wine. The leaves are used for thatching huts and making hats and mats. Fibers are used for making wicker furniture and as thread for weaving. Some trees are valued for lumber.

Palm oil provides one of the greatest eco-nomic benefits from this plant. Carnauba wax comes from a palm in Brazil. The wax is extracted from leaves and boiled seeds.

Date palms produce delicious fruit that has been enjoyed over many centuries. (*P. dactylifera,* cultivated in southeastern California, has even tastier fruit than *P. canariensis.*) Ancient civilizations had many uses for this fruit, the most important of which was in making delicious confections. King Solomon was said to have revered the tree.

COMMON NAME: *Palmetto, Cabbage*
BOTANICAL NAME: *Sabal palmetto*
FAMILY: Palmae (Palm)

DESCRIPTION: Cabbage palmetto has a large, unbranched trunk (approximately 1½ feet in diameter) and grows 50 to 80 feet tall. The leaves are large (4 to 7 feet long and nearly as wide) and fan-shaped and spread around the top of the tree. Each leaf has many thin spiny segments, which are long and drooping. Small white flowers occur in clusters in early summer. The fruit is a small, round black berry.

ORIGIN: In nature cabbage palmettos are found along the coast from the southern part of North Carolina, South Carolina, and Georgia and throughout Florida, including the Keys.

HOW TO GROW: Cabbage palmetto, or sabal palm, is adaptable and can be grown in moist or dry conditions, in full sun or partial shade. They look good planted together in a border or singly as a specimen tree. Cabbage palmetto is hardy only in zones 9 and 10.

The species name, *palmetto,* is from the Spanish word *palmito,* meaning "little palm," which is somewhat of a misnomer since the tree grows to a height of 80 feet or more. Other common names include Carolina palm and swamp cabbage.

Palmetto leaves are folded into many segments. This is an adaptation designed to store water in times of drought and to reduce water loss during dry seasons.

The large leaf buds of *S. palmetto,* when eaten in a salad, are said to have the same flavor as cabbage, thus the common name. Early Florida Indians used this part of the tree so much that it became a staple in their diet.

(Unfortunately the practice of removing the leaf buds eventually kills the trees.) Raccoons and some birds feed on the small berries.

The soft wood can be crosscut and polished to make unusual and beautiful tabletops. The wood is also used for dock pilings, poles, broom handles, and baskets. Fibers from the young leaf-stalks are fashioned into brooms and brushes.

Palm oil has many uses in addition to its culinary value. The oil is also used to make wax, sugar, alcohol, and fiber. It can be found in such diverse products as candles, detergents, and lubricants for jet engines.

The state seal of South Carolina includes the cabbage palmetto to commemorate its role in the Revolutionary War. In Charleston, American forces built a stockade from cabbage palmetto, and on June 28, 1776, General William Moultrie defeated British ships in Charleston Harbor.

Cabbage palmetto is the palm commonly distributed in churches on Palm Sunday. It is the state tree for both South Carolina and Florida.

COMMON NAME: *Paloverde, Blue*
BOTANICAL NAME: *Cercidium floridum*
FAMILY: Leguminosae (Pea)

DESCRIPTION: The small tree has a short trunk and open, spreading branches. The leaves are few and far between, and the tree actually remains leafless for most of the year. When found, the leaves are thick and pale blue-green. The bark is very smooth and also has a blue-green tint to it. The flowers, which come in late spring and again in late summer, are bright yellow. The topmost petal is usually spotted with red. The anthers (which contain the pollen) are also red. *C. microphyllum*, yellow paloverde, is a closely related species. This species has a yellowish green trunk and does not grow quite as tall as *C. floridum*.

ORIGIN: Blue paloverde is native from central and southern Arizona to southeastern California.

HOW TO GROW: In nature paloverde is most often found along washes and valleys. It is sometimes found on desert grasslands. Because it grows quickly, paloverde is sometimes used for erosion control.

The name paloverde is derived from two Spanish words, *palo* and *verde*, meaning "green tree" or "green pole."

Photosynthesis in paloverde is actually performed by the green branches and twigs, as the leaves appear only briefly. The leaves develop during the rainy season of spring and then fall as soon as they mature. By having leaves on the tree for such a short time, the tree exposes less surface area to the sun, thereby more efficiently conserving moisture.

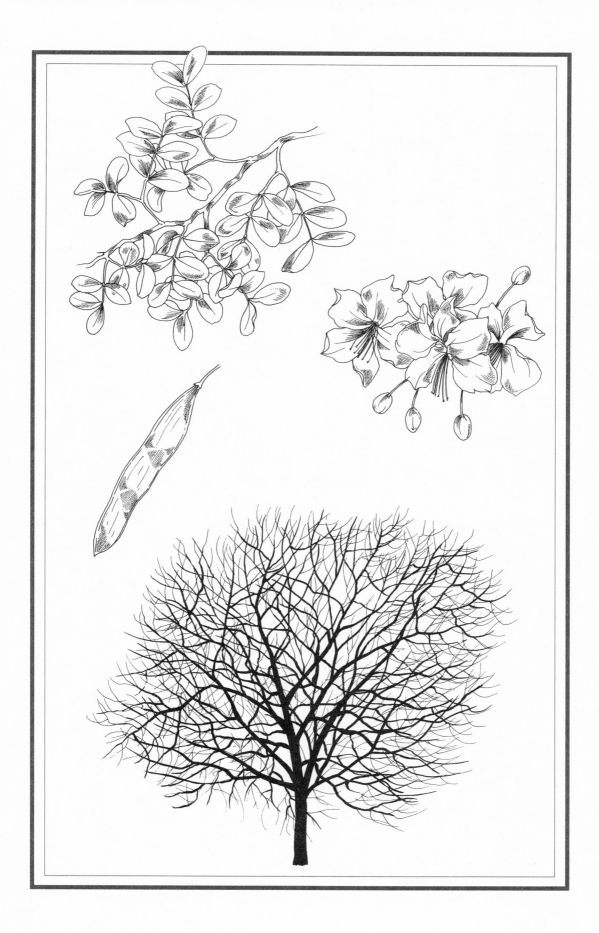

The leaves go almost unnoticed because they appear at the same time as the brilliant golden flowers, which cover the entire tree. The trees are sometimes referred to as *lluvia de oro*, Spanish for "shower of gold."

Paloverde wood is close-grained and not very strong and of medium weight, 34 pounds per cubic foot. The sapwood is a nice clear light yellow.

The immature seed pods were eaten by the Indians, who also ground the mature seeds into meal.

Wildlife feeds on all parts of the tree. Deer browse the twigs and pods. These parts sometimes provide emergency rations for domesticated animals as well. Several kinds of birds and rodents eat the seeds, and the flowers provide pollen for making an unusually good honey.

Blue paloverde is the state tree of Arizona.

COMMON NAME: **Pawpaw**

BOTANICAL NAME: *Asimina triloba*

FAMILY: Annonaceae (Annona)

DESCRIPTION: Pawpaw is considered a large shrub or small tree. It grows to a height of about 30 feet, with a trunk measuring 8 inches in diameter. The bark is dark brown and is covered with small warts. The long, narrow leaves are borne on slender stems and occur in two rows. The leaves are green on top, paler green underneath, and turn yellow in autumn. When bruised or crushed, the leaves emit a strong, unpleasant odor. The flower, which appears in early spring, is 1½ inches long and has three outer petals, which can be green, brown, or purplish. The fruit is small and curved and somewhat resembles a small banana.

ORIGIN: Pawpaw is native from southern Ontario and New York south to the panhandle of Florida, west to Texas.

HOW TO GROW: Pawpaw trees need rich, moist soil. They are hardy to zone 5.

Pawpaw was first reported by the DeSoto expedition in the lower Mississippi valley in 1541. Pawpaw is in the same family as several tropical fruit trees including Annona, custard-apple, sugar-apple, and soursop. The name pawpaw is a corruption of the name of the tropical fruit tree, papaya, which is not even related. The tasty fruit of pawpaw is edible and has the consistency of custard. It is sometimes used as a gentle laxative. Generally today the fruit is eaten only by wildlife such as opossums, squirrels, and raccoons.

The seeds, which are poisonous, were sometimes ground into a powder and put on the heads of children who had lice. The leaves, also, were thought to have insecticidal properties.

The name *Asimina* is an American Indian name. The species name, *triloba,* means "three-lobed," refering to the configuration of the flower. The wood is not often used commercially but is worked well with tools and offers opportunities for various crafts.

COMMON NAME: *Pear*

BOTANICAL NAME: *Pyrus* sp.

FAMILY: Rosaceae (Rose)

DESCRIPTION: Pears are lovely deciduous trees bearing white flowers in spring. The leaves are alternate and stalked. Many species are valued for their fruit (differing technically from an apple only in the number of "grit cells" per fruit). Other species and varieties produce no fruit but make exceptional ornamental trees. *P. calleryana* 'Bradford' is one of the best known of the pears. It grows to be 50 feet tall and is distinctly triangular in its growth form. The leaves are glossy green, turning brilliant scarlet or purple in autumn. During spring the tree is covered with a cloud of white blossoms, but no fruit is produced. Grows in zones 5 to 9. *P. salicifolia,* willowleaf pear, has long, slender leaves and grows 15 to 25 feet tall. Grows well in zones 4 to 7. *P. communis* is the well-known fruit tree, now naturalized in many areas. The flowers are white, composed of rounded petals, and the fruit has green or brown skin and thick, juicy meat.

ORIGIN: *P. calleryana* originated in China. *P. salicifolia* and *P. communis* are native to northeast Asia.

HOW TO GROW: Pears need full sun but are otherwise adaptable to a wide range of environmental conditions. They do not do well in extremely wet or dry soils or in highly alkaline soils, but they tolerate relatively infertile soil, air pollution, drought, and wind. Container-grown or balled trees can be transplanted in spring. Young trees need ample moisture to become quickly adapted.

Pears have been cultivated for many centuries. They were probably introduced to the United States by European gardeners when the colonies were established. Missionaries in California and Mexico were responsible for introducing pears there.

Pears are the second-largest fruit crop in the world, exceeded only by apples. World produc-

tion of table and dessert pears exceeds 7 million tons annually. More than half of the world production is grown in Europe. Italy leads the world market in pears. In France more than half the pears grown or imported are used to make perry, a sparkling alcoholic drink made from fermented pears.

For the ambitious and adventuresome gardener, pears can be grown in narrow-necked bottles that are then filled with brandy for an unusual "ship-in-a-bottle" sort of conversation piece. When young pears begin to form on the trees, a clear glass bottle is slipped over the immature fruit. If the bottle is then given sufficient support so that it will not pull the fruit off the tree, the pear continues to grow and mature. When fully ripe, the pear is pulled off the tree and is firmly (and amazingly!) ensconced within the bottle.

COMMON NAME: *Persimmon*

BOTANICAL NAME: *Diospyros virginiana*

FAMILY: Ebenaceae (Ebony)

DESCRIPTION: Persimmon trees grow between 20 and 70 feet tall. The pointed leaves are 4 to 6 inches long, shiny green on the upper side, lighter green underneath. The bark is dark brown with deep fissures and rather chunky looking. Fragrant white flowers are borne in June, male and female flowers occurring on separate trees. The yellowish or purple-brown fruit, which ripens in autumn, is an inch across.

ORIGIN: Common persimmon grows from Connecticut to southern Florida, west to central Texas, and north to Iowa.

HOW TO GROW: Persimmon trees are useful in the city as they tolerate urban pollution. Although the trees perform well in either alkaline or acidic soils, the soil must be well drained. Persimmon needs full sun. Grows in zones 4 to 8.

The name *Diospyros* means "fruit or wheat of the gods"; *virginiana* means "from Virginia." Other common names include bara-bara, boawood, butterwood date plum, and 'possum wood. This last name was given to the tree because opossums find the fruit so tasty. Songs and stories indicate that many a 'possum hunt ended at the bottom of a 'simmon tree.

Persimmons are in the same family as the tropical tree ebony, and it is sometimes known as ebony of America. The name is easily explained by the heartwood, which is such a dark brown that it looks nearly black. The wood weighs 59 pounds per cubic foot and is extraordinarily strong and heavy. It shrinks greatly while drying and cracks while being cured unless seasoned correctly. Persimmon sapwood is used to make the heads of golf clubs. In the textile industry manufacturers of shuttles estimate that a persimmon shuttle can be used for

1,000 hours of work without being replaced.

There are few words to describe the extraordinarily tart taste of a green persimmon. After eating one of these little fruits, one's face tends to stay puckered up for hours. Captain John Smith, recounting the pilgrims' experience with persimmons near Jamestown, Virginia, said, "If it be not ripe, it will draw a man's mouth awrie with much torment." So strong is this flavor that it is said it may take a full day to erase the taste of a green persimmon.

The immature fruit has a high tannin content and is astringent. Tea made from the fruits was used as a gargle for sore throats and thrush. It was drunk sparingly for heartburn, diarrhea, and upset stomachs. Warts and cancers were treated with this tea as well.

As tart as the green fruit is, the ripe fruit is considered quite tasty, comparable to the taste of dates. Ripe persimmons are used in making cakes, puddings, and beverages. American Indians made persimmon bread and dried the fresh fruits like prunes. In the wild the fruits are eaten by many kinds of birds and wildlife, including opossums, raccoons, skunks, deer and songbirds.

Cooking oil, extracted from the seeds, has a flavor similar to that of peanut oil.

COMMON NAME: *Pine*

BOTANICAL NAME: *Pinus* sp.

FAMILY: Pinaceae (Pine)

DESCRIPTION: Pines have a wide range of physical characteristics and grow anywhere from 10 to 100 feet tall. Generally they have a single unbranching trunk from which lateral branches occur in whorls or tiers. The leaves are needlelike and occur in clusters of three to five, encased in a parchmentlike substance at the base of the leaves. Male flowers produce pollen, often in great clouds; female flowers develop the cone. Pines are usually conical in shape when young and then develop rounded tops with age. *P. bungeana*, lacebark pine, grows to be 50 to 60 feet in height. Several trunks give it an interesting form. The exfoliating (peeling) bark creates beautiful and unusual markings on the tree trunk. Native to China, it is hardy in zones 5 to 8. *P. contorta*, beach (or shore) pine, grows well in Pacific coastal regions but not as well along in the eastern part of the country. It has many branches and is rounded at the top, growing only 30 feet tall. Native from Alaska to California. *P. parviflora*, Japanese white pine, grows 60 feet tall and has graceful, spreading branches. The cones are 3 inches long and egg-shaped. Although it is sometimes unattractive when young, it develops into a lovely specimen tree if given time. Native to Japan, it grows in zones 5 to 7. *P. strobus*, eastern white pine, grows to be 150 feet tall and is prized for its use as timber. The leaves are long and soft, and the cylindrical cones measure 5 to 7 inches long. This species is intolerant of salt spray or urban pollution. Native to eastern North America, it grows in zones 4 to 7. Pinyon pines grow at high elevations (usually between 2,000 and 9,000 feet). There are three main species of pinyons—*P. cembroides*, Mexican pinyon; *P. monophylla*, singleleaf pinyon; and *P. edulis*, nut pinyon, the

most common species. It is a relatively short, scrubby tree, rarely reaching over 30 feet in height, and is commonly found in the south rim of the Grand Canyon.

ORIGIN: See Description.

HOW TO GROW: Success with pines is dependent on choosing a species that grows naturally in your area or is well adapted to the growing conditions of your garden. Generally pines prefer light, very well-drained soil. They are sensitive to drying winds and burn easily from winter sun. The roots, in particular, are sensitive to drying out and should not be exposed to the air. When transplanting, keep the roots covered with soil at all times. Various species tolerate different conditions. For example, Japanese white pine tolerates salt spray, and Austrian pine tolerates air pollution.

When settlers first moved to northeastern America, the eastern white pine forests were so vast that legend claimed a squirrel could travel all of its life without ever coming down from the trees. Without disturbance from man, eastern white pine, *P. strobus,* can grow as long as 400 years.

The trees, however, are frequently disturbed by man, for eastern white pine is greatly prized by carpenters because it works easily and finishes nicely. Early pioneers and colonists built homes and churches from the wood. So valuable was the wood that the British crown at one time declared that the largest white pines must be reserved for mast wood for the Royal Navy. The colonists took great offense at the British crown's claiming their trees, and they often poached the trees at night. An early colonial flag included the image of a white pine, and in the seventeenth century the state of Massachusetts placed this same image on a coin.

Native Americans often used the bark of white pine as medicine. The bark was most often soaked in water and then placed on wounds as a dressing. Extracts from the inner bark treated diarrhea and coughs. A concoction made from the gum relieved pain from arthritis.

In many parts of this country, Scotch pine, *P. sylvestris,* is best known at Christmas time when it is brought indoors to be decorated. It's usefulness, however, has greatly increased over

the past two decades, particularly in reforestation projects. Because of its hardiness and quick growth habit, it survives conditions that other trees cannot tolerate.

Scotch pine was introduced to this country from Eurasia. During the 1800s tar from the tree was used in making many kinds of medicines, in particular, those used to treat skin disorders such as eczema and psoriasis. The needles were made into a stuffing, called "pine wool," which was thought to help repel pests such as lice and fleas.

Lodgepole pine, also known as black pine, scrub pine, shore pine, coast pine, and tamarack pine grows along the West Coast. The name lodgepole was given to this tree because tall, light poles were made from the lumber.

Lodgepole pine benefits from burning as the closed cones are released by fire, freeing the seeds to be carried by the wind. It never grows very big around, 3 feet being about the maximum. The wood has been used for poles and fence rails and for making sheds, barns, and small bridges.

Longleaf pine, *P. australis,* is also called turpentine pine because the sap from this tree provides great quantities of turpentine and pine oil, an important ingredient in cosmetics and perfumes. The wood is used for making railroad ties and for the manufacture of pulpwood and craft paper.

Pinyon nuts were ground into flour by both pioneers and American Indians. The wood was also used for firewood and for making houses and fence posts. Archaeologists have found crude utensils made from the wood of pinyon pine. The wood, with its pungent aroma, is a popular ingredient in commercial incense. Resin from the wood was once used as caulking for boats.

Pinyon is one of the most important native noncultivated nut trees in the United States. The nuts can be eaten raw, roasted, or put into candies. Autumn harvests result in great quantities of the nuts, which are quickly bought by local residents and by gourmet food shops. Pinyon trees make popular Christmas trees in the Southwest.

When English settlers first arrived on the southern coasts of the United States, they found loblolly pine, *P. taeda*. The name loblolly was given to this large pine species because of where it grew—in muddy, murky areas. The word *loblolly* is actually an Old English word meaning "porridge," the name given because the murky breeding ground for the pine trees looked like thick gruellike porridge.

The rounded crown of loblolly pine is cause for its characteristic "moan" as the wind goes through the trees. This tree was also sometimes called rosemary pine because of its pungent fragrance.

Early pioneers used resin drained from loblolly pines in many ways: as an ointment, as a rope preservative, as a sealant for roofing paper, and as caulking for boats. Turpentine, another product derived from the trees, was used for lamp oil and as a preservative and sometimes even as an external medicine.

Today loblolly pine is used in making low-grade brown paper and plywood. It is considered by many to be the most economically important eastern and southern forest tree.

P. aristata, bristlecone pines, are short, scrubby, incredibly old trees—thought to be the oldest known living plants. One tree is supposedly more than 4,600 years old. The needles of this unusual tree persist for twenty to thirty years, as opposed two to three years exhibited by other conifers. Many of these ancient trees are protected in the Inyo National Forest near Bishop, California.

Many states have chosen different species of pines as their state tree: red pine—Minnesota, longleaf—Alabama, ponderosa—Montana, shortleaf—Arkansas, western white—Idaho, eastern white—Maine and Michigan. Singleleaf pinyon is the state tree of Nevada, and the nut pinyon is New Mexico's tree.

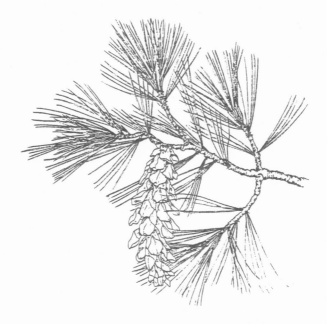

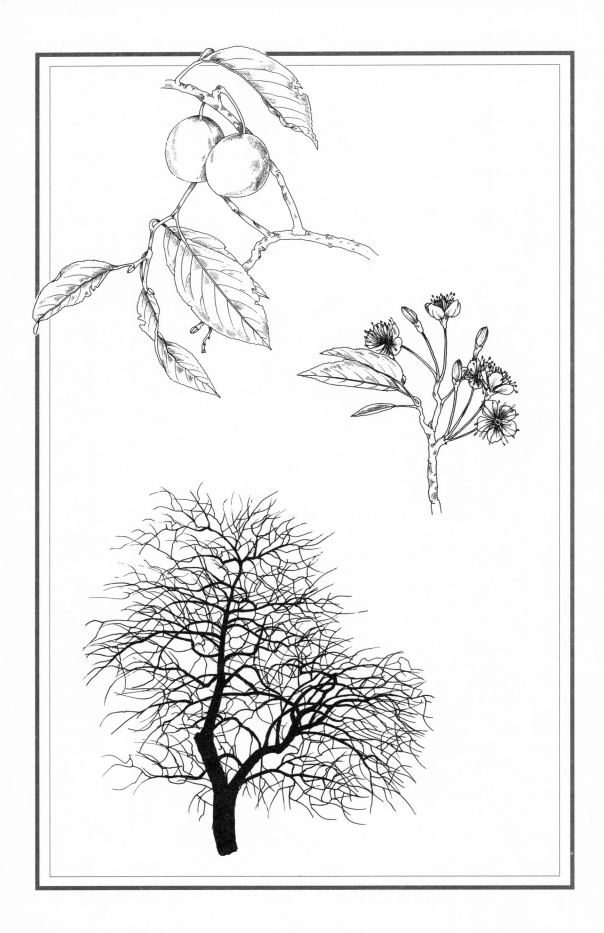

COMMON NAME: *Plum, American*

BOTANICAL NAME: *Prunus americana*

FAMILY: Rosaceae (Rose)

DESCRIPTION: Plum trees not only provide abundant fruits, they are also prized as ornamental trees. In spring, before the leaves come out, large, showy white flowers appear. The flowers, which measure nearly an inch across, are made up of five rounded petals. The fruit that follows is also about an inch in diameter and has thick red skin, sour meat, and a large stone. The tree reaches a height of about 30 feet and has a short, stout trunk and many spreading branches. Some of the many cultivars of this species include 'Blackhawk', 'Hawkeye', and 'De Soto'. It is hardy to zone 4.

The wood is hard and strong. The heartwood is a rich, red-brown color.

ORIGIN: American plum is originally from an area stretching from southeastern Saskatchewan east to New Hampshire, south to Florida, west to Montana and Oklahoma.

HOW TO GROW: In nature plums are found in moist valley soils and low slopes. The trees grow in full sun and benefit from soil rich in organic matter. The plants should be watered regularly at least until the young trees have become established, then watered only in very dry times.

Many cultivars have been developed from the wild American plum tree. Some horticulturists list more than 300 named varieties. The new strains have greatly improved flavor over that of the original fruit. The wild fruit, though tart, has always been used to make jellies, jams, preserves, and pudding. American Indians, particularly the Dakota, Omaha-Poncas, and Pawnee Indians, considered the wild plum to be an important food source.

Not only was the fruit enjoyed, but the wood, too, was used. Slender branches were tied together to make brooms, and the bark was boiled and made into a poultice to treat skin disorders. The Navajo Indians made a red dye from the root, a practice still followed by artists today.

During the mid-1800s, Lieutenant James Abert worked for several different railway companies. It was his job to find routes across the continent for the railroads to follow. In September 1853 he wrote in his diary that he and his companions found "a quantity of luscious plums." They were traveling in southern New Mexico, and the heat was nearly unbearable. The fruit of the plum finally quenched their thirst and made it possible for them to continue with their journey.

Today, because the tree grows so rapidly and spreads its roots quickly, it is sometimes grown for erosion control.

COMMON NAME: *Princess-tree*

BOTANICAL NAME: *Paulownia tomentosa*

FAMILY: Scrophulariaceae (Foxglove)

DESCRIPTION: The impressive princess-tree grows 40 to 50 feet tall and has large, thick branches with an open growth form. The leaves are broad and heart-shaped, measuring 5 to 10 inches long. The flowers look like small fox-gloves, not surprisingly, for the two plants are closely related. The blossoms of princess-tree are lilac colored with darker spots and inner yellow stripes. The flowers appear in clusters 10 to 12 inches long in spring before the leaves emerge.

ORIGIN: China (naturalized from New York to Georgia)

HOW TO GROW: Princess-tree needs full sun or partial shade and rich, well-drained neutral to acidic soils. Plant from balled or container-grown plants in early spring. It grows rapidly and withstands urban pollution and spray from salt air. The flowers, leaves, and fruits may cause a litter problem. Can be grown in zones 6 to 9.

The common name princess-tree as well as the genus were named in honor of Anna Paulowna (1795–1865) of Russia, princess of the Netherlands. Other common names include Empress-tree and Royal Paulownia. Also called tung tree, this species was mentioned often in the Chinese classics. The Chinese valued it for its ornamental beauty as well as for its high-quality lumber.

Although princess-tree contains substances that may be toxic, it has been used as food and medicine for centuries. The Chinese made the leaves into a hair ointment, which was thought to be effective in preventing baldness and slowing the graying process.

In the United States, a wash was made from the leaves to bathe sore and tender feet, and the inner bark, soaked in whisky, was used to treat fevers. Liver ailments were sometimes treated with a mixture of princess-tree flowers and other herbs. Liquid obtained by crushing the leaves was used to get rid of warts.

Today, the light-weight wood is exported to Japan, where it is made into furniture and specialized items such as sandals.

Tung oil, derived from the princess-tree, is sometimes used as a substitute for linseed oil in paint and varnish for a better waterproof finish.

COMMON NAME: *Privet*

BOTANICAL NAME: *Ligustrum japonicum*

FAMILY: Oleaceae (Olive)

DESCRIPTION: Privet can be either deciduous or evergreen. It has closely growing branches, giving a compact, dense appearance. Japanese privet grows 6 to 10 feet tall and has small round leaves. 'Variegata' has leaves that are edged with white or light yellow. The shrub puts out flowers, which are not always desired. Prune early in spring to avoid flowering.

ORIGIN: native to Japan and Korea

HOW TO GROW: Privet is used in hedges or as a foundation plant. It withstands air pollution, drought, and heavy shearing or pruning. For best results grow in full sun or partial shade in any kind of soil that drains well.

Privet was first brought to this country from Europe as a hedge plant. In warm areas the plant is considered evergreen, making it particularly desirable as a living screen. Because it grows so quickly, it is ideal to clip to create topiary.

Medicinally, privet has been quite useful for more than a hundred years. Privet flowers placed directly on the forehead supposedly relieved a headache. The berries were used as a laxative, the leaves as a mouthwash and gargle. Concoctions made from the leaves and flowers helped to treat menstrual disorders.

A yellow dye is made from the bark, a green and black dye from the berries. Baskets were sometimes woven from pliable branches.

Privet is a symbol of defense according to the English language of flowers.

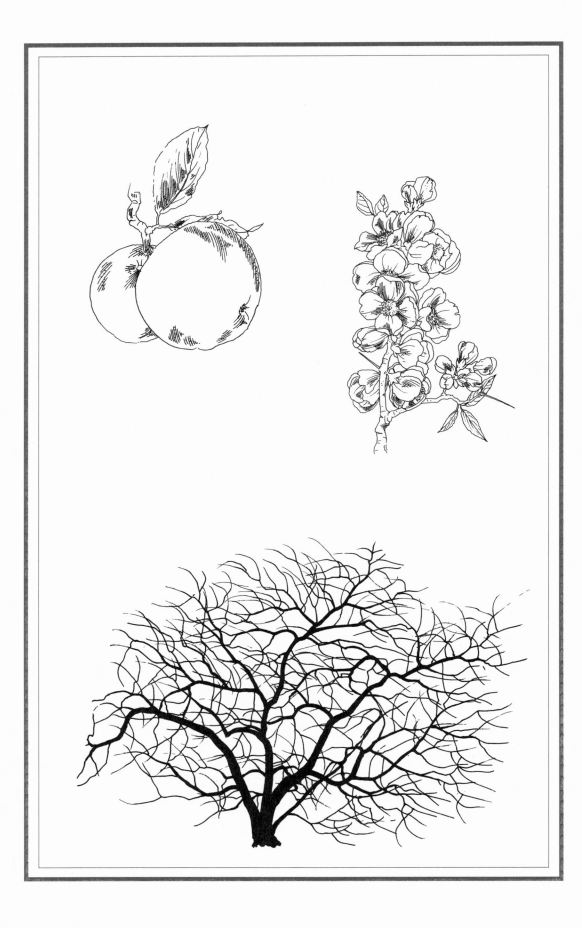

COMMON NAME: *Quince, Flowering*
BOTANICAL NAME: *Chaenomeles speciosa*
FAMILY: Rosaceae (Rose)

DESCRIPTION: One of the earliest and most beautiful of the spring-blooming ornamental shrubs, flowering quince puts forth blossoms long before the foliage appears. The deciduous shrub grows 6 to 10 feet tall. The flowers are large and attractive, looking somewhat like apple blossoms, and appear in all shades of pinks and reds as well as white. The fruit is pear-shaped and ripens in fall. Other species include *C. japonica* and *C. x superba*. A closely related plant is quince, *Cydonia oblonga*. The blossoms, which come in late spring, are either pink or white and sweetly scented.

ORIGIN: native to China

HOW TO GROW: Quince can be trained on a wall where it can grow as tall as 10 feet, or it can be left as a freestanding shrub. Pruning keeps the shrub at any height desired. It tolerates a wide range of soil conditions as long as it is well drained, and it is happy under a variety of light conditions from full sun to full shade. This hardy shrub grows well as far north as zone 5.

Flowering, or Japanese, quince is indigenous to China and is used extensively in Japan as a potted plant. It was taken to Europe and then later made its way into American gardens via the European plant market. Records in Colonial Williamsburg list it before 1775. Today it is a very popular plant to use in bonsai.

French gardeners in particular have found flowering quince to be useful as a landscaping plant. They sometimes planted entire hedges of the shrub, the dark red, pink, and white blossoms adding great color and charm to the early spring landscape.

True quince, *Cydonia oblonga*, is native to Kashmir. From there it was taken to Cydonia on the island of Crete. When quince was later grown in Athens, Greek gardeners kept the name *Malus Cydonia*—apple of Cydonia. The name quince is actually a corruption of the name Cydonia, hav-

ing changed from Cydonia to *cooin*, then *quyne*, and finally quince.

The quince fruit preserved in honey flavored food and wine. The fruit was thought to hold power as a love charm as well as protection against the "evil eye." The power of the fruit was thought to be so strong that they sometimes painted quinces on the sides of buildings, just as the Pennsylvania Dutch painted hex signs on the sides of barns. This symbolism persisted in England through the Victorian age when a box of quince fruit was thought to be a token of love and affection.

During the Middle Ages the fruits were often grown in gardens and espaliered on outdoor walls. They were used extensively in cooking and as flavoring for sauces, beverages, and preserves.

COMMON NAME: *Redbud, Eastern*

BOTANICAL NAME: *Cercis canadensis*

FAMILY: Leguminosae (Pea)

DESCRIPTION: Eastern redbud is an attractive small deciduous tree. At maturity it reaches a height of 35 feet. The leaves are broadly oval, measuring almost 4 inches across, with a pointed tip. The numerous small flowers (½ inch long) are bright pinkish red and appear in early spring. Cultivars are available with white or double flowers.

ORIGIN: native from New York to Florida, west to Texas

HOW TO GROW: Eastern redbud needs sandy well-drained soil. It tolerates sun or shade, acidic or alkaline soils but does not do well in heavy, clayey soils. Grows in zones 5 to 8.

The tree is commonly called Judas tree because according to legend, after Judas betrayed Christ, he hanged himself on *C. siliquastrum,* a tree closely related to the eastern redbud, which grows in western Asia and southern Europe. The legend further contends that the blossoms were originally all white and turned bright pink in shame.

Eastern redbud is at its most beautiful in early spring when the branches are covered with lilac-pink blossoms even before the leaves emerge. Not only are the blossoms beautiful to look at, they are also tasty to eat! (Try them raw in salads or fried for an unusual appetizer.) Folk healers used the bark to treat diarrhea and sometimes even as a remedy for leukemia. American Indians made bows from the wood of the western redbud, *C. occidentalis.*

Redbud is the state tree of Oklahoma.

COMMON NAME: *Redwood*

BOTANICAL NAME: *Sequoia sempervirens*

FAMILY: Taxodiaceae (Baldcypress)

DESCRIPTION: *S. sempervirens* is the only species surviving from a very ancient genus. Redwoods are massive evergreen trees, reaching a mature height of up to 300 feet. They have a thinner trunk than giant sequoias and usually measure only about 28 feet in diameter. The oblong leaves are ¼ inch long and resemble those found on hemlock.

ORIGIN: In the fog belt, northern California and southern Oregon, growing for miles along the coast and only 25 miles inland

HOW TO GROW: Redwoods do not grow well in the eastern United States, but are considered a useful landscape tree on the West Coast. They need full sun and plenty of room. Well-drained, deep neutral soil and thorough watering of young trees results in optimum growth, sometimes as much as 3 to 5 feet per year when young. This species of sequoia needs the right combination of fog, rainfall, humidity, and warm temperatures. It rarely grows well outside California and Oregon, zones 8 to 10.

The genus *Sequoia* was named for Chief Sequoia, the half Cherokee Indian who created an alphabet for his people living in the Appalachian mountains.

Redwood trees are very resistant to rot. In Redwood National Park, fallen trees stay intact for many years, which makes the creation of hiking trails through the park quite challenging. Because the redwood grows in the fogbelt where the soil is always moist, danger from forest fires is greatly reduced.

The durability of redwood makes it attractive in the lumber market. Everything from caskets to cigar boxes are made from this wood. Other items include boats, shingles, and pipes.

One of the tallest, if not the tallest, tree in the world is a redwood that is 368 feet tall.

Annual ring counts on some species have shown that redwoods can live to be as old as 2,200 years.

Walt Whitman wrote of the death of a redwood:

In the echo of the teamsters' calls and the clinking chains, and the music of choppers' axes,

The falling trunk and limbs, the crash, the muffled shriek, the groan,

Such words combined from the redwood-tree, as of voices ecstatic, ancient and rustling. . .

The redwood is the state tree of California.

COMMON NAME: *Rhododendron*

BOTANICAL NAME: *Rhododendron catawbiense*

FAMILY: Ericaceae (Heath)

DESCRIPTION: There is tremendous variation within the *Rhododendron* genera. The shrubs range from tiny dwarf species to tree-sized specimens. Flowers generally occur in clusters and are either bell- or trumpet-shaped. Flowers come in all colors except for blue and black. The *Rhododendron* genus includes the azaleas, many of which are deciduous; otherwise, the shrubs are evergreen. The native catawba rhododendron is a small tree (up to 20 feet) with a rounded crown and beautiful purplish pink blossoms. The flowers are 2½ inches across and appear in late spring and early summer. Zones 5 to 8. *R. chapmanii* is 6 to 8 feet tall and has pale pink flowers coming in late spring. Zones 5 to 9. *R. fortunei* grows 12 feet tall and has fragrant pale purple to pink flowers in late spring. Zones 6 to 9. *R. maximum* grows 12 feet tall and has pale rose or white blossoms in early to midsummer. Zones 4 to 8.

ORIGIN: *R. catawbiense* is native from southern Virginia south to northern Georgia and northeastern Alabama.

HOW TO GROW: Rhododendrons need, even demand, acidic soils. They perform best in light shade but tolerate full shade as well, though blooming may be somewhat reduced. The soil should be rich in organic matter and moist. Prune plants after flowering to maintain an attractive shape. Rhododendrons will perform best if they are fed infrequently.

The leaves and flowers of all rhododendrons are poisonous. Honey made from the nectar, too, is toxic. In spite of, or maybe because of, its toxicity, rhododendron was once taken in minute quantities to treat heart disease. American Indians used the crushed leaves in a poultice to treat pain from arthritis and headaches.

Probably because it is poisonous, rhododendron is a symbol of danger.

COMMON NAME: *Russian-olive*

BOTANICAL NAME: *Elaeagnus angustifolia*

FAMILY: Elaeagnaceae (Oleaster)

DESCRIPTION: Russian-olive has an interesting, irregular shape. It grows to a height of 12 to 20 feet and is covered with silvery gray willowlike leaves throughout summer and autumn. Both twigs and undersides of the leaves are distinctly silvery. Half-inch thorns appear along the small twigs and branches. The fragrant flowers are silver on the outside, yellow on the inside. The dark brown bark peels in long strips. The tree is deciduous. *E. pungens* 'Fruitlandii', thorny elaeagnus, is an attractive cultivar, which also bears bright red edible fruit.

ORIGIN: *E. angustifolia* is native to Europe and western Asia.

HOW TO GROW: Russian-olive needs full sun or partial shade but tolerates poor, dry soil and high winds. The plant performs best when essentially ignored. Too much water and fertilizer creates an unattractive, lanky growth. Regular pruning helps to maintain an attractive growth pattern. It grows in zones 2 to 7.

Russian-olive is also known as thorny oleaster, wild olive, and silver berry. It is not related to the true olive, *Olea europaea,* although the leaves do look similar.

The fruit from Russian-olive is eaten by songbirds such as cedar waxwings, grosbeaks, robins, and quail.

The tree grows so quickly that it is sometimes considered a pest. It is tolerant to air pollution, cold, and drought.

COMMON NAME: *Saguaro*
BOTANICAL NAME: *Cereus giganteus*
FAMILY: Cactaceae (Cactus)

DESCRIPTION: Saguaro, a tree cactus, is a tall column with a spiny trunk and two to ten spiny, erect branches. It grows to a height of 20 to 35 feet, the trunk reaching a diameter of 2 feet or more. Both the trunk and branches bear sharp gray spines. Flowers appear in late spring and sometimes again at the end of the summer. They are composed of several waxy white petals, which occur at the tips of the branches, and they smell somewhat like melons.

ORIGIN: Saguaro is native from Arizona south to Mexico. Local populations are sometimes found in southeastern California.

HOW TO GROW: Giant cactus is found only in nature on south-facing slopes in sandy desert soils.

Native Americans used the fruit both fresh and dried, making it into preserves and beverages. The "ribs" provided wood for shelters, fences, and kindling. The woody tissue in the stem is so strong that it has been used for hundreds of years in constructing houses and buildings.

There are no leaves on the cactus, and food is made in the thick green stems. To absorb as much moisture as possible in its desert habitat, the saguaro sends out a tremendous number of shallow roots (some roots have been traced as far as 40 feet from the stem). The shallow root system quickly absorbs the infrequent desert rains and sends the water to the trunk and branches, where it is stored.

During periods of extreme drought, the upright branches, or "arms," droop and may even curl a little, creating the illusion of the branches hugging the stem. In older trees the branches may never regain their upright position.

Although the sharp spines keep most wildlife away, Gila woodpeckers and gilded flickers make their nests in rounded holes at the tops of the branches. Other birds follow once these nests have been abandoned. Elf owls and cactus wrens in particular make use of these old nesting spots. The seeds from the cactus are eaten by various kinds of wildlife including white-winged doves.

The cactus blooms after the spring rainy season, in late April and May. The blossoms open slowly over a period of about two to three hours, starting about eight o'clock in the evening. The large, heavy blossoms measure about 2 to 3 inches across. The fruits come about a month later. The fruits were a staple food for the Arizona Indians. The Papagos even date their New Year from the time of fruiting of the saguaro. The fruits were made into jam, jelly, or preserves.

Saguaro cactus grows amazingly slowly. A plant 4 inches tall may be about eight years old, and at the ripe old age of twenty, it may be only 10 inches tall. It is difficult to determine the age of a cactus, but botanists believe that saguaros live to be about 150 years old.

This tree is also known as *Carnegiea gigantea*.

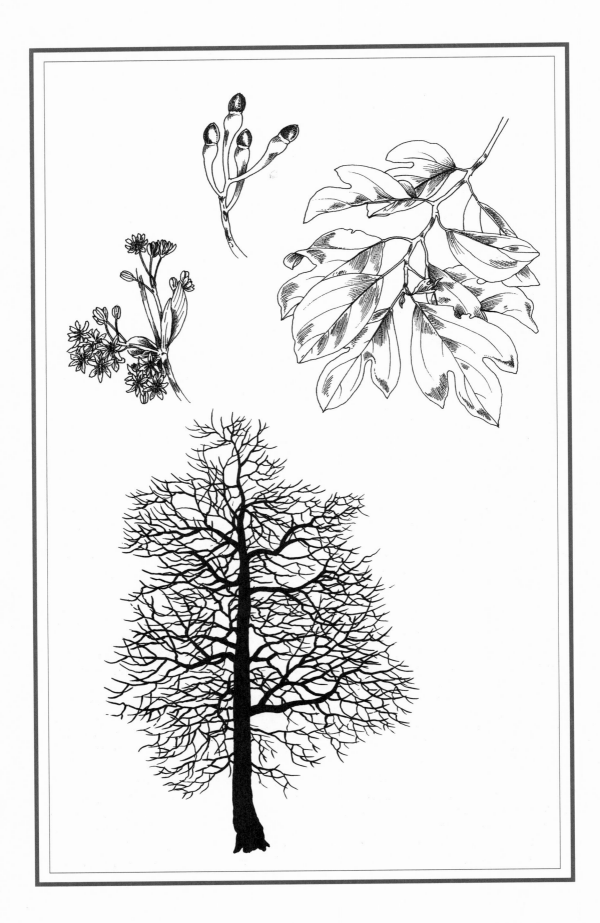

COMMON NAME: *Sassafras*

BOTANICAL NAME: *Sassafras albidum*

FAMILY: Lauraceae (Laurel)

DESCRIPTION: A distinguishing characteristic of sassafras is its leaves, which come in three distinctly different shapes. They are either entire (the leaf edges smooth and uninterrupted), have one lobe off center (resembling a mitten), or have two small lobes to either side of center. The tree can grow to a height of 60 feet. It has reddish brown furrowed bark, and the leaves turn orange and red in fall. Flowers, which come in spring, are small and yellowish green. The seeds are dark blue and about the size of a pea.

ORIGIN: eastern United States from Maine to Florida

HOW TO GROW: Sassafras trees look wonderful naturalized in the garden along with other native trees and shrubs. The foliage—dark, cool green in summer and brilliantly colored in fall—provides for nice background color in the garden. The trees grow in virtually any kind of garden soil and in a variety of light conditions from full sun to dappled shade. Small sassafras trees can be transplanted, but this is not always a wise decision because the taproot is extraordinarily long and is difficult to dig up. Better propagation methods include transplanting small suckers or planting freshly ripened seeds. If the seeds are stored and planted at a later time, they should undergo cold stratification—that is, packed between layers of organic matter (such as sphagnum moss) and placed in the refrigerator for about four months.

The name sassafras is an American Indian name adopted by early European explorers. Sassafras is sometimes called cinnamonwood because Spanish explorers who first saw the tree growing in Florida mistook it for a cinnamon tree. This mistake is with us still.

Not only does sassafras have three different kinds of leaves, it also has three different kinds of fragrances. The leaves have a distinctly citrus fragrance, the wood has a medicinal odor, and the roots smell like root beer.

The sweetly scented roots were used as a commercial flavoring for many years, primarily in the manufacturing of root beer and tea. Researchers during the 1960s, however, discovered that the oil from sassafras caused liver cancer in rats (if given in tremendous quantities); consequently, the FDA outlawed its use for internal medicine or flavoring.

Early settlers, blissfully unaware of the potential damage that sassafras could impart upon laboratory rats, drank great quantities of sassafras tea with only beneficial results. Both Indians and pioneers used sassafras tea as a stimulant and to calm fevers and spasms caused by illness. It was also sold as a cure for rheumatism.

The reputation of sassafras tea increased to a fever pitch during the nineteenth century until sassafras roots eventually became a major export of this country. At one point it ranked second only to tobacco in exportation.

Although no longer used internally, sassafras tea is still used as an external ointment, which is particularly effective in relieving the irritating itch from poison-ivy rash.

COMMON NAME: *Sequoia, Giant*

BOTANICAL NAME: *Sequoiadendron giganteum*

FAMILY: Taxodiaceae (Baldcypress)

DESCRIPTION: Giant sequoias have the greatest trunk diameter of any tree in the world, up to 80 feet. Their height is also tremendous, sometimes measuring up to 250 feet. They look very much like the redwoods. The leaves are small and needlelike, the cones only 2 to 3 inches long.

ORIGIN: central California, particularly at elevations of 5,000 to 8,000 feet.

HOW TO GROW: Sequoias are particular about their environmental conditions and have a relatively small growth range. On the West Coast it is an important landscape tree. It is considered hardy in zones 7 to 9 and semihardy in zone 6.

Giant sequoias are the second-oldest living organisms (bested only by bristlecone pines). They are even more ancient than redwoods. A felled tree showed annual rings indicating an age of approximately 3,200 years. They are among the tallest of all trees, often reaching a height of 250 feet, and are the largest in diameter, sometimes measuring 80 feet around or more.

Giant sequoias go through an extraordinarily long growth cycle. Generally the trees only begin their flowering cycle after one hundred years. During the first year the trees produce pollen, and cones are created. The seeds within the cones take at least another year to mature. The mature seeds may remain viable within the cones for up to twenty years. In spite of the tremendous size

of a mature tree, it takes approximately 3,000 seeds to make up one ounce. (Unlike redwoods, trees do not sprout from old stumps or fallen logs. All new growth is from seeds.)

The pigment that is released with the seeds has baffled scientists for years, as chemicals within it allow it to be used as a dye or an ink, which will not fade.

Although the wood is relatively brittle, the trees are amazingly sturdy. Fallen trees are thought to last more than a thousand years.

So massive are giant sequoias that it is estimated that a single tree could provide enough lumber to build 150 five-room homes. Luckily they are protected by law, and commercial use of the trees is prohibited. Efforts by early natu-

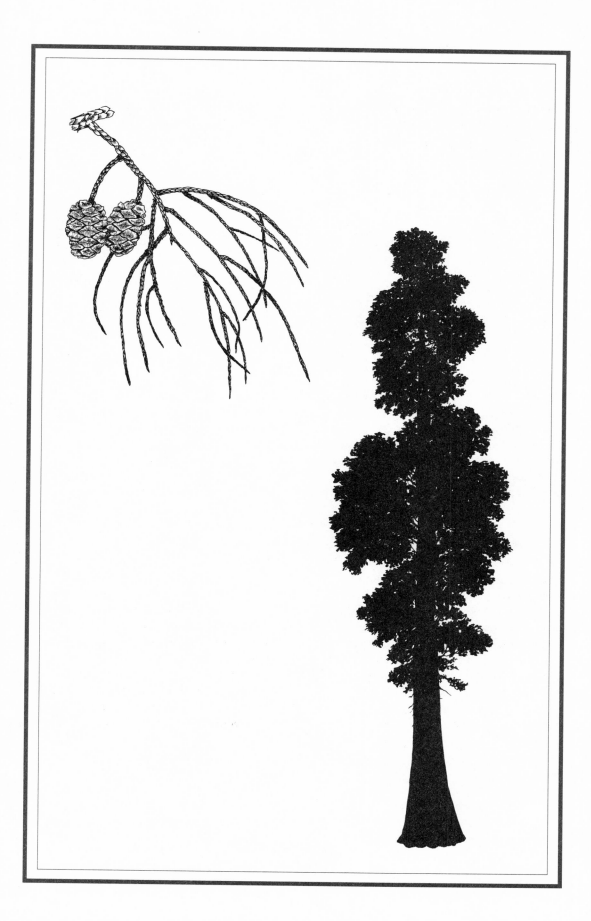

ralists and conservationists were successful in saving one fourth of the total original giant sequoia forests. Almost all the remaining giant sequoias are protected in Yosemite, Kings Canyon, and Sequoia national parks.

COMMON NAME: *Serviceberry*

BOTANICAL NAME: *Amelanchier laevis*

FAMILY: Rosaceae (Rose)

DESCRIPTION: The leaves of this species of serviceberry are only half-grown at the time of flowering. As they mature, the leaves become whitish underneath. The flowers are composed of white petals measuring ¾ inch in length. There are about twenty-five species of deciduous shrubs and trees in this genus.

ORIGIN: found from central Alaska to western Minnesota, south to Colorado, and west to northern California

HOW TO GROW: Serviceberry does not tolerate drought conditions but grows well in the garden if given sufficient moisture. It grows in zones 5 to 8.

The berries from this shrub are made into pies and sweet breads and are sometimes dried like raisins. Tea made from serviceberries mixed with other herbs was taken by American pioneer women to control excessive menstrual bleeding. Cherokee Indians used a similar solution as a digestive aid. Children with worms were treated to a bath of serviceberry tea

All kinds of wildlife, including birds, bears, and squirrels, enjoy the fruit.

In the western part of the country, a similar species, A. *florida,* or Pacific shadblow, grows. The tree was given the name shadblow because it was thought that when serviceberry began to bloom, the shad begin to run. An old-fashioned name for this is "sarvis."

The small fruit, which appears in summer, was a staple in the diet of many Indian tribes in the west. The wood, because it is straight and slender, was used to make arrow shafts.

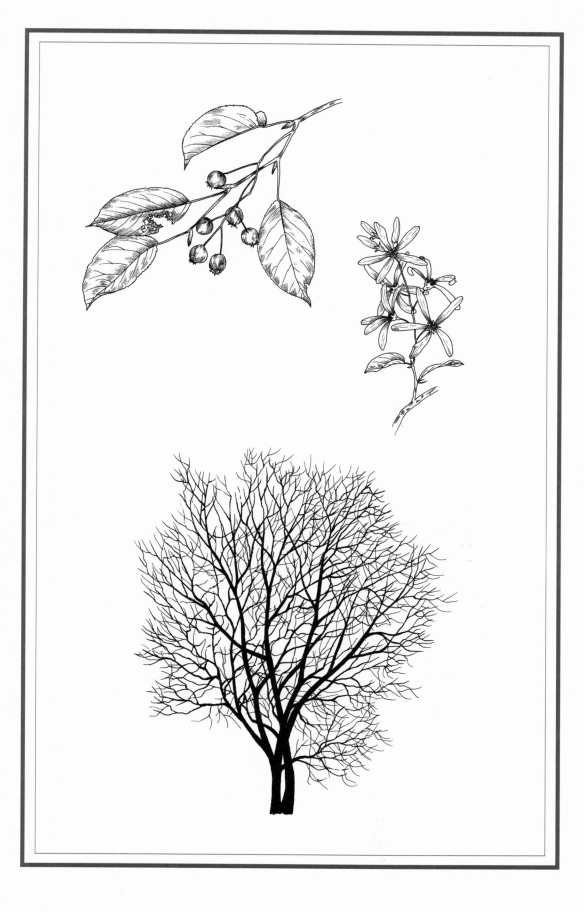

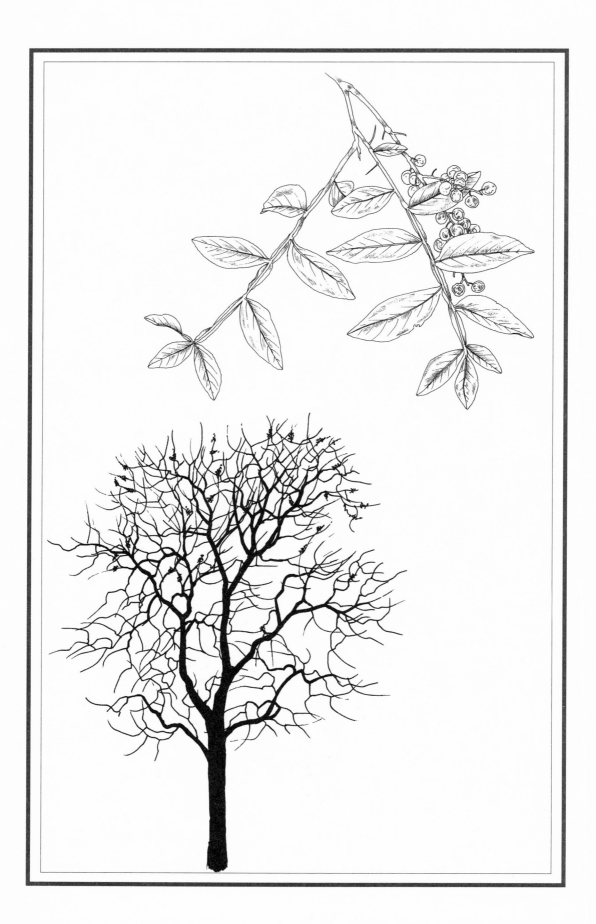

COMMON NAME: *Soapberry, Western*

BOTANICAL NAME: *Sapindus drummondii*

FAMILY: Sapindaceae (Soapberry)

DESCRIPTION: Soapberry is a small tree or shrub with open, upright branching that reaches a height of 20 to 40 feet. The leaves are pinnately compound and occur in eleven to nineteen leaflets. The leaves are yellowish green on top and slightly hairy underneath. The light gray bark is smooth when young, becoming rough and fissured with age. The small yellowish white flowers come in late spring or summer. The leathery, transparent yellow fruit has a single dark brown seed.

ORIGIN: The shrub is native from Missouri south to Louisiana, west to southern Arizona, and northeast to Colorado.

HOW TO GROW: In nature soapberry grows along streams or in other moist soils. It is often found in the border between hardwood forests and clearings.

All parts of this tree are considered poisonous, particularly the fruit. In spite of its toxic nature, however, the fruit was used by early American settlers to treat rheumatism and kidney disease. Containing saponin, the fruits have been used for centuries as a substitute for laundry soap, even though sap from the fruit may cause skin irritation in some people. Substances from the fruit are used to make varnish and floor wax.

The hard, strong wood of this tree is very heavy, weighing 52 pounds per cubic foot. The sapwood is white, the heartwood a light brown. Although the wood is hard, it splits easily, which made it ideal to make cotton pickers' baskets and frames for packs. It was also a popular material for making baskets.

The dark brown round seeds are sometimes made into necklaces, buttons, and even rosaries.

Western soapberry is also known as wild Chinatree, because the fruits were mistakenly thought to be those found on the Chinaberry tree.

COMMON NAME: *Sourwood*

BOTANICAL NAME: *Oxydendrum arboreum*

FAMILY: Ericaceae (Heath)

DESCRIPTION: Sourwood trees grow 40 to 50 feet tall. The leaves are long (3 to 8 inches) and oblong, turning early in the fall to a brilliant scarlet-purple color. The flowers appear in mid-summer and are borne in long graceful racemes. The entire appearance of the tree is of graceful layering. The fruits appear in fall and are found in a light gray capsule.

ORIGIN: native to the United States from Pennsylvania and Illinois to Florida and Louisiana

HOW TO GROW: Sourwoods need moist, well-drained soils high in acidity (pH of 4.5 to 5.5). Although sourwood grows well in the shade, both fall color and summer flowers will be superior if the tree is located in full sun. It is quite sensitive to air pollution. Grows in zones 5 to 9.

The name sourwood comes from the acrid taste of its leaves. It is also known as arrow-wood, elk tree, lily-of-the-valley-tree, sorrel gum, sorrel-tree, and titi tree.

Sourwood is most often grown as an ornamental tree, particularly for its outstandingly beautiful autumn foliage. It is usually not grown for its wood, which is extremely close and hard and therefore difficult to work with tools.

Concoctions made from the sap of the tree were used in treating fevers. The bark was chewed to soothe pain from mouth ulcers, and tea made from the leaves was useful in treating such diverse ailments as diarrhea, indigestion, and dysentery.

Perhaps the best-loved use of sourwood is in lending its sweet fragrance to incomparable sourwood honey.

COMMON NAME: *Spicebush*

BOTANICAL NAME: *Lindera benzoin*

FAMILY: Lauraceae (Laurel)

DESCRIPTION: The spicebush shrub grows to a height of 6 to 17 feet. The flowers are composed of 6 identical petals and sepals and appear in early spring. Male and female flowers occur on separate plants. The leaves, when crushed, emit a pleasant, fragrant, spicy odor.

ORIGIN: Spicebush occurs from Maine south to Florida, west to Texas, and north to Missouri.

HOW TO GROW: Spicebush prefers rich, moist soils and thrives at the edges of woods in indirect sunlight. It grows in zones 2 to 10.

Spicebush, also known as Benjamin bush, is sometimes called "forsythia of the wild" because of its attractive yellow flowers. American Indians used spicebush extensively as a medicine. They made the berries into tea to treat coughs and croup, measles and cramps, and to bring on a late menstrual period. Taken straight, the berries were used to treat flatulence and colic. The crushed berries were used to relieve pain from bruises or in athritic joints. Tea made from the bark was thought to be good as a tonic to improve the blood.

Sometimes the early pioneers dried the berries and ground them into a fine powder as a substitute for allspice.

COMMON NAME: *Spruce*

BOTANICAL NAME: *Picea* sp.

FAMILY: Pinaceae (Pine)

DESCRIPTION: In general spruces have a single, unbranched trunk. Lateral branches form tiers or whorls. Needlelike leaves are square and can be rolled between the fingers, unlike the needles of the fir tree, which are flat. *P. abies*, Norway spruce, is considered the most widely cultivated evergreen tree in North America. It grows fairly rapidly and quickly reaches a height of 60 to 80 feet, spreading 20 to 30 feet. It grows conical in shape. The mature cones are long, measuring nearly 6 inches in length. *P. glauca*, white spruce, looks much like the Norway spruce but has smaller cones and does not grow as tall. Although this species tolerates heat and wind relatively well, it does need a period of cold during the winter months and is therefore not suitable for growing in many southern climates. *P. pungens*, Colorado spruce, has silvery blue foliage and grows to a height of about 80 feet. Lower branches of this species typically age and die. Lower branches are also often subject to canker, mites, and bagworms.

ORIGIN: White spruce is native to northern North America, Colorado spruce to the Rocky Mountains, Norway spruce to Europe.

HOW TO GROW: Spruces are best established in the yard or garden if planted from container-grown or balled and burlaped plants. When planting, avoid exposing the roots for more than a few minutes. The trees should be planted in full sun or partial shade and in soil that is evenly moist, acidic, and well drained. Mulching helps to maintain an even level of moisture. White spruce is the hardiest and most tolerant species. It survives winter temperatures down to minus seventy degrees and summer heat up to one hundred degrees. In the landscape spruces are used successfully as single specimen trees or in groups to create a screen.

White spruce, *P. glauca*, is also known as Adirondack spruce and skunk spruce. The reason for the latter name is that if the needles are bruised, they emit an unpleasant skunklike odor. White spruce has long, even fibers and is prized for manufacturing of paper. The wood is also used to make piano sounding boards, violins, and other musical instruments, and for making furniture, lightweight oars, and canoe paddles.

There is a symbiotic relationship between spruces and the bird called the spruce grouse.

Spruces supply the specific requirements of the grouse while the grouse helps to maintain the spruce. Neither can live without the other. Other wildlife is not as kind to spruce trees. Moose, deer, and rabbits browse on the young growth, and bears and porcupines strip the bark from the trees to get to the sapwood.

Not only is wood from the spruce tree trunk valuable, the young pliable roots of white spruce were also used extensively. Native Americans used them as cords or twine, and in particular as laces for their canoes.

Black spruce wood was used to make fish barrels and top masts for ships. Red spruce is a resilient and straight-grained wood often used to make stringed instruments.

Although red and white spruce are sometimes used for Christmas trees, they are not always satisfactory because they tend to drop their needles in a warm, dry room.

"Spruce beer," a nonalcoholic beverage, was made from boiling the young leafy twigs of red and black spruce. Flavoring and sweetening were added to the concoction to make a drink tasting something like soda water. It was often drunk to combat scurvy. Old-fashioned chewing gum was also made from resin derived from black and red spruce.

The inner bark was used to treat kidney stones and rheumatism. Pitch from red, white, and black spruce trees was used in manufacturing oil-based paints and in varnish and medicines.

Black spruce is so named because, from a distance, the trees look black and charred, owing to the short, brown hairs that cover the entire tree. In Maine young forests of black spruce are called "black growth." The Alaskan taiga, where black spruce is found in great numbers, comes from the Russian word *taiga*, which means "land of little sticks," because of the appearance of the black spruce.

Resin droplets from spruce and fir trees are natural air pollutants. Sunshine reflecting and refracting from these droplets actually creates a temperature inversion, which cuases a subtle haze in the air. This blue haze was the reason for the name "blue ridge" given to mountains in Virginia.

Blue spruce is the state tree of Colorado and of Utah. Black Hills spruce is the state tree of South Dakota.

COMMON NAME: *Sumac, Smooth*

BOTANICAL NAME: *Rhus glabra*

FAMILY: Anacardiaceae (Cashew)

DESCRIPTION: Sumac is either a large shrub or a small tree, growing to a height of 20 feet. The leaves are pinnately compound, about 12 inches long. The small white flowers appear in clusters, and the fruit is truly spectacular. Dark red berries are clustered together and covered with short, sticky red hairs. The berries ripen in late summer and persist through winter.

ORIGIN: Smooth sumac is the only tree or shrub native to all the contiguous forty-eight states.

HOW TO GROW: Sumac grows in full sun and likes well-drained soil. It tolerates drought conditions but performs better if watered during the hot summer months. In nature sumac is found in forest borders, in new clearings, roadsides, and waste places.

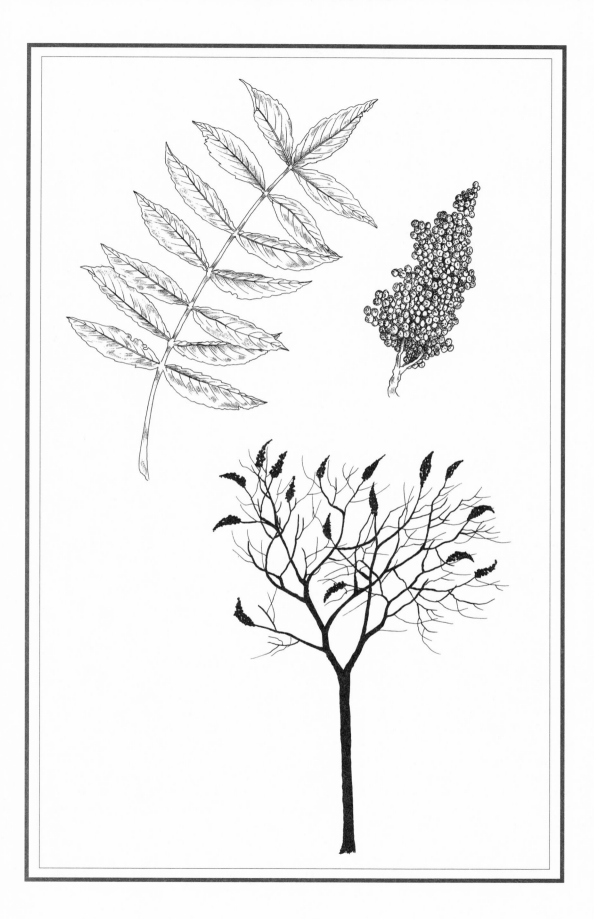

American Indians ate the raw young sprouts of smooth sumac. The tart seeds were used to flavor drinks (tasting somewhat like lemonade) or chewed to quench thirst. *R. integrifolia* is even called lemonade sumac. Many birds and small mammals feed on the berries during winter.

Smooth sumac was used medicinally for a variety of purposes. The leaves were smoked to control asthma attacks. Tea was made from the leaves to treat asthma and diarrhea. Tea made from the bark was used primarily to treat digestive disorders but was also sometimes drunk to relieve mouth sores and to break fever.

Great care should be taken not to confuse smooth sumac with poison sumac, which has white berries and untoothed leaves and is highly poisonous.

COMMON NAME: *Sweet Gum*

BOTANICAL NAME: *Liquidambar styraciflua*

FAMILY: Hamamelidaceae (Witch-hazel)

DESCRIPTION: Sweet gum leaves are star-shaped and closely resemble maple leaves. The tree grows to 75 feet tall. The young twigs and branches sometimes have corklike ridges. The fruit, spiny balls full of resinous sap, is large and interesting. During fall the leaves turn brilliant shades of yellow, purple, or red.

ORIGIN: native from Connecticut west to Missouri and Illinois and south throughout Florida and Texas, all the way to Mexico

HOW TO GROW: Sweet gum trees need full sun or partial shade and prefer acidic soils. Although sweet gum needs shelter from high winds, it tolerates salt spray. It grows in zones 5 to 9.

The genus name *Liquidambar* refers to the gold-colored sap from the tree. Other common names include alligator-tree and alligator wood (because of the rough bark), hazel pin, incense tree, satin walnut, red gum, or sap gum. The name sweet gum is from the pleasant odor of the sap, which is used in France to scent gloves.

The wood is used most often as a veneer, but it is also used to make pulpwood, barrels, and boxes. The resinous sap taken from the trunks of the trees was used to make gum, which was used medicinally as well as for chewing gum.

The unseasoned wood from this tree is very dense and heavy, weighing about 37 pounds per cubic foot. Because it takes so long to properly season the wood, the trees are sometimes girdled and left standing for a year before being felled.

A closely related tree, Oriental sweet gum, *L. orientalis*, produces a sweetly scented resin, storax, which is used commercially in perfumes and medicines and to flavor soft drinks, candy, and chewing gum.

Gum from the tree was chewed to ease sore throats, coughs and colds. An ointment made

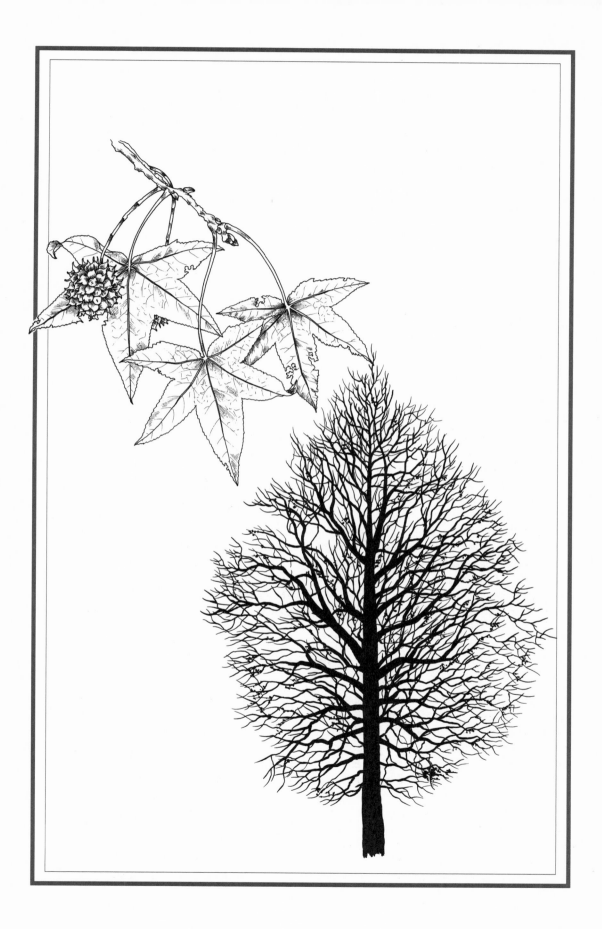

from the plant was applied externally on sores, cuts, wounds, and skin disorders. The inner bark, boiled in milk, was thought to be effective for treating diarrhea.

In the southern United States, folks would dip twigs of sweet gum in whiskey and chew them to cure diarrhea. The gum, mixed with lard, was used to treat skin disorders.

COMMON NAME: *Sycamore*

BOTANICAL NAME: *Platanus occidentalis*

FAMILY: Platanaceae (Sycamore)

DESCRIPTION: Sycamore can grow to be a massive tree with a large straight trunk and a multitude of crooked branches. It grows to be 75 to 100 feet in height and often spreads to an equal width. The bark is smooth and whitish. It peels to reveal interesting brown or gray places beneath. The fruit, which appears in fall, is a single brown ball with many spines, hanging from a slender stalk and often persisting through winter. The leaves are 5 to 8 inches long and 4 to 9 inches wide, having shallow pointed lobes. California sycamore, *P. racemosa*, has whitish, smooth bark and a barrel-shaped trunk.

ORIGIN: Maine south to Florida, west to Texas and Nebraska

HOW TO GROW: Although in nature sycamores are often found growing close to water, along streams, or at the edges of lakes and swamps, the trees are adaptable to a wide range of environmental conditions. They need full sun and moist, well-drained soil and are excellent to use as shade trees where the landscape is open enough to accommodate them. They tolerate a great deal of pruning and are easy to transplant, even at a mature stage. Sycamores are hardy to zone 4.

The species name *occidentalis* means western. Other common names include buttonball and buttonwood, which refer to the round little fruit, and American planetree, referring to its resemblance to the Oriental planetree, and water beech, in reference to its preferred habitat. It is also sometimes called ghost tree because of its mottled white bark. The bark was made into tea used to treat measles, coughs, and colds.

Sycamore has a more massive trunk than any other eastern native hardwood tree. The tree holding the record for the largest trunk measures

more than 11 feet in diameter. The genus name *Platanus* is from the Latin name for the Oriental planetree.

Sycamore wood is used for specialty items such as furniture parts, butcher blocks, particleboard, and fiberboard. It is also sometimes used to make railroad ties and fence posts. The heartwood averages 34 pounds per cubic foot and experiences a great deal of shrinkage while being cured. Because it warps easily, the wood is difficult to season.

In some parts of the United States, sycamore

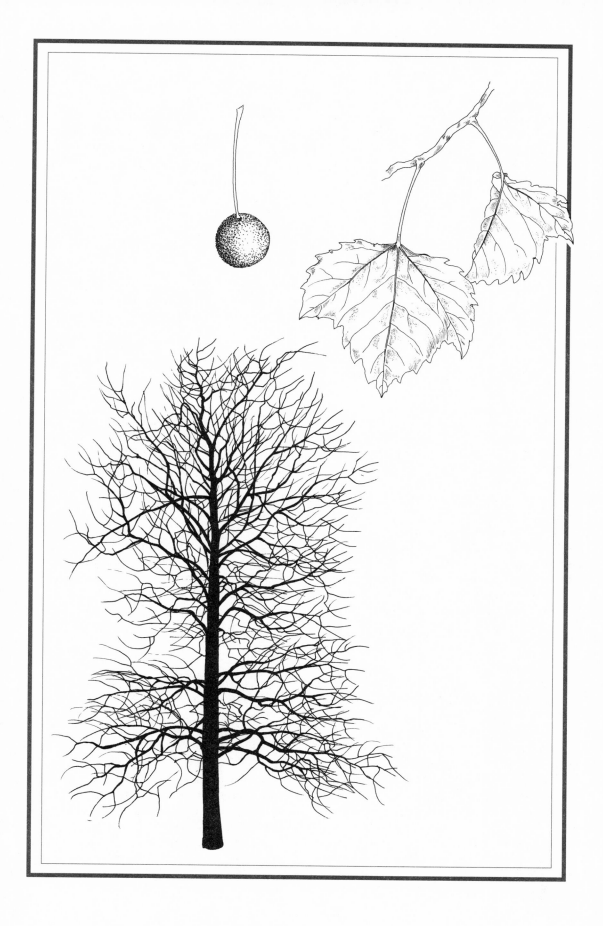

trees are grown as an agricultural crop, with the trees planted close together in straight rows. They are allowed to grow until they reach a height of 9 to 10 feet, at which time they are cut with a giant mowing machine that slices the trees off at the stump. New trees then regrow from the stump.

Sycamores are relatively effective as air cleaners. The surface area of the foliage collects dust in the air, and the leaves are able to take 25 to 30 metric tons of dirt per hectare from the air. Eventually rain washes the dirt from the leaves and deposits it back into the earth.

COMMON NAME: *Tamarack*
BOTANICAL NAME: *Larix laricina*
FAMILY: Pinaceae (Pine)

DESCRIPTION: Tamarack has thin, open branching. It grows to a height of 40 to 80 feet and has a trunk diameter of 1 to 2 feet. The foliage is composed of soft deciduous needles that appear in clusters. The needles are a blue-green color, turning yellow in autumn before they drop. The ½- to ¾-inch-long cones are a lovely rose-red color. Western larch, *L. lyallii*, has thick bark and leaves that occur in clusters of thirty to forty. The leaves are needlelike and are pale blue-green, turning bright yellow in autumn.

ORIGIN: Tamarack is found across the northern part of North America, growing from Alaska east to Labrador and south to New Jersey. Local populations are found in West Virginia and Maryland.

HOW TO GROW: In nature tamarack is found in wet bogs and swamps or sometimes in loamy soils in upland areas. The species *laricina* is hardy to zone 2.

In addition to eastern larch, other common names for *L. laricina* are hackmatack, American larch, and black larix.

Tamarack is useful as an ornamental plant in extremely northern climates because it is so hardy. The roots often grow at right angles. American colonists took advantage of the bent roots to make necessary joints in boats and to connect the deck timbers to the ribs.

Native Americans used the new, slender roots to attach birch-bark strips in their canoes. The best roots for this purpose came from beaver ponds, as these roots were particularly slender and pliant.

Tamarack lumber was used for railroad cross-ties, for house framing, and for poles and pulpwood. *L. decidua* is the source of an important and valuable turpentine.

Tea made from the bark of larch had many medicinal uses. It served as a gargle for sore throats and was drunk as a laxative or a general tonic. Applied externally, the tea was thought to be good for headaches. Made into a poultice, the bark treated sores and burned skin. The gum was chewed for indigestion.

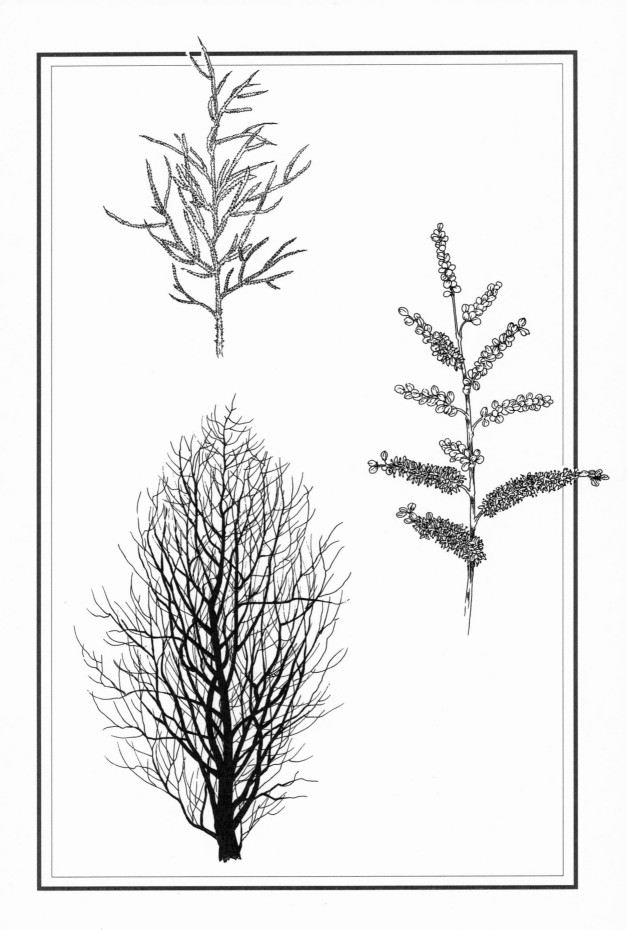

COMMON NAME: *Tamarisk*

BOTANICAL NAME: *Tamarix chinensis*

FAMILY: Tamaricaceae (Tamarisk)

DESCRIPTION: Tamarisk is a small deciduous tree or shrub with thin, spreading branches.
It grows to a height of 16 feet, and the trunk
attains a diameter of only about 4 inches. The
blue-green leaves are needlelike, narrow, and
pointed. The reddish brown bark is smooth,
eventually developing deep ridges. Small clusters of light pink flowers come in spring and
summer. *T. ramosissima* 'Rosea' is a cultivar
boasting beautiful sprays of bright pink flowers.
Against the blue-green leaves, the blossoms add
great beauty and interest to the garden. This
species, which is only 8 feet tall, can be grown in
zones 2 to 8. It actually prefers infertile soils and
tolerates salt sprays.

ORIGIN: Native to Asia and southeastern
Europe, tamarisk is naturalized from southwest-
ern Nebraska west to Nevada and south to
Texas and California.

HOW TO GROW: In nature tamarisk
grows best in wet, open areas, such as stream
banks or irrigation ditches. The trees tolerate
both alkaline and salty soils.

The genus name *Tamarix* is probably a reference
to the Tamaris River in Spain. Other common
names are saltcedar and or five-stamen
tamarisk.

Tamarisk was first grown in this country for
erosion control and as an ornamental shrub. It
adapted quickly to growing conditions here and
is now considered a weedy pest, although large
populations of tamarisk are useful in providing
cover for wildlife such as deer. It develops very
deep roots and uses a great deal of water. It is
very difficult to eradicate, as the shrub produces
many seeds, which are quick to germinate, and
cuttings, which grow quickly.

COMMON NAME: *Tulip Poplar*

BOTANICAL NAME: *Liriodendron tulipifera*

FAMILY: Magnoliaceae (Magnolia)

DESCRIPTION: Tulip poplars grow to be nearly 100 feet tall. When grown in the open, branching occurs throughout the tree. In the forest, growing close to other trees, branches generally occur only high up in the trees. The leaves are deeply lobed but blunt across the top. They turn bright yellow in fall. The trees do not produce flowers and fruit until they reach the age of about ten. The large and showy flowers have six greenish white petals with orange bands toward the base and bright orange stamens. Because the flowers are only borne high in the tree, they often go unnoticed until they fall to the ground.

ORIGIN: native to eastern United States from Ontario to Florida and west to Wisconsin

HOW TO GROW: Tulip poplars put forth a massive root system and therefore need plenty of deep, rich, well-drained soil. The trees grow best in full sun and slightly acidic soils. Plant in spring from balled or container-grown plants. They should be watered and mulched during periods of drought. The trees are generally hardy and easy to grow but are susceptible to damage from aphids and from injudicious use of herbicides. They grow in zones 5 to 9.

Other names for this tree are yellow-poplar, whitewood, tulip tree, canary wood, and canoe wood.

Tulip poplar is considered one of the most valuable hardwood trees native to the eastern half of the United States, with varied applications such as furniture, musical instruments, and veneers. It is also used in cabinetry to make sashes, doors, and shelves. Tulip poplar is particularly prized in the hat industry because it does not absorb moisture from steaming.

Early colonists from Virginia introduced tulip poplar to Europe. It has been recorded that pioneers hollowed out a single log from a massive tulip poplar tree to make a canoe.

American Indians made a tea from the bark to treat upset stomach, rheumatism, and fever. The tea was also an ingredient in several home cough remedies used by early American settlers. A solution made from the bark applied externally treated fractured limbs, cuts, and insect and snake bites. The leaves, crushed and made into a poultice, alleviated headache. An ointment made from the buds soothed burns and skin disorders. Pieces of green bark were chewed as a general stimulant or an aphrodisiac.

Tulip poplar is the state tree of Indiana, Kentucky, and Tennessee.

COMMON NAME: *Walnut, Black*

BOTANICAL NAME: *Juglans nigra*

FAMILY: Juglandaceae (Walnut)

DESCRIPTION: Black walnut grows to be 70 to 90 feet tall with a trunk diameter of 2 to 4 feet. The pinnately compound leaves measure 1 to 2 feet long. During summer the leaves are dark green, turning a golden yellow in autumn. The bark is dark gray with deep ridges resulting in a diamond-shaped pattern. The fruit is a sweet, delicious nut covered with a green or brown husk ripening in October or November.

ORIGIN: native throughout most of the eastern half of the United States from Massachusetts south to Florida

HOW TO GROW: Black walnut needs full sun but tolerates partial shade. It does best in moist, well-drained soil. It is hardy to zone 5.

The genus name *Juglans* is Latin, meaning "Jupiter's nut." The species name *nigra* means "black." The name walnut comes from the German name *Welshnuss,* or "foreign nut."

From a culinary point of view, black walnut is considered very valuable. The nuts are a flavorful ingredient in making cakes, sweets, and ice cream.

As lumber, black walnut is much coveted and is thought to be the most valuable timber wood in North America. Records show that a thousand board feet once sold for $25,000. So valuable is the wood that black walnut trees are sometimes stolen from suburban yards for their fine timber.

Once it has been seasoned, the wood shrinks very little and responds to being cut and finishes very well. It is used for making gunstocks because it retains its shape well, helps absorb the recoil from the gun, and is lightweight.

The wood is greatly prized for its beauty, particularly by woodworkers. The heartwood is very dark, but is even more beautiful because of

spots of pale yellow sapwood. The wood is used for furniture and veneer.

During the mid-1800s walnut wood was used to make waterwheels (because of its resistance to decay), charcoal for gunpowder, and railroad ties, which were made from the trunks. Oil extracted from the nuts was used in hair oil and as butter.

In addition to the lumber, the tree is valued for its delicious nuts and for a dye made from the husks. In earlier days the dye was used to color wood, cloth, and human hair. The green shucks give off a pigment used in brown hair dyes. A cap of walnut hulls was sometimes worn to keep hair from turning gray or to restore it back to a darker color if gray hair had already crept in. The dark bark, in addition to the husks of the nuts, is used to make a yellow dye.

Some folks believed that carrying a walnut would prevent rheumatism. The bark, which helped to staunch the flow of blood, was often used by soldiers during the Civil War. The oil from the nuts, soaked into a cloth, was used to stop the pain of toothache, and a salve was made from the leaves. The walnut was also thought to cure the insane.

Black walnut trees produce the chemical juglone, which prevents the growth of other trees close by, even young seedlings of the same species. This natural herbicide prevents the healthy growth of such plants as tomatoes (as far away as 80 feet), alfalfa (up to 60 feet), pota-toes, apples, blackberries, rhododendron, and pines. This botanical characteristic is called allelopathy.

Walnuts have apparently been cherished for centuries. In Pompeii archaeologists unearthed stores of walnuts, presumably destined for a special feast or celebration that was rudely inter-rupted by the eruption of Mount Vesuvius.

COMMON NAME: *Waxmyrtle*

BOTANICAL NAME: *Myrica cerifera*

FAMILY: Myricaceae (Waxmyrtle)

DESCRIPTION: Waxmyrtle, also called bayberry, is an evergreen shrub growing 10 to 20 feet tall with fragrant wedge-shaped leaves hav-ing resin dots on both the top and lower sur-faces. The berries, wax-covered nutlets, appear from August through October. Northern bay-berry, *M. pensylvanica,* is similar but is not ever-green. *M. californica* is called Pacific waxmyrtle. It grows nearly 30 feet tall and has saw-toothed leaves. The berries are showy and attractive; the foliage shiny and evergreen. Myrtle warblers and other songbirds feed off the berries.

ORIGIN: southern waxmyrtle is native from New Jersey south to Florida and west to Texas.

HOW TO GROW: Waxmyrtle performs best in full sun or partial shade when grown in dry, sandy soil. Berries are produced only when male and female plants are grown close together. Spring pruning helps to keep the plant attractive looking. It grows in zones 7 to 9.

Waxmyrtle was first found by Adelbert von Chamisso, who (in spite of his German-sounding name) was a French botanist and explorer. He arrived in San Francisco on a Russian ship in 1805 and is credited with finding both waxmyr-tle and the California poppy. Other names for waxmyrtle are southern bayberry, waxberry, and candleberry.

Early colonists extracted the wax from the berries by dipping them in boiling water. The wax was then made into fragrant candles.

Tea made from the root bark was good for relieving stomach disorders and also for treating ulcers, scrofula, and jaundice. For dry, itchy skin, myrtle tea was thought to be particularly soothing. The dried, powdered root was included with many other dried herbs to make a tea drunk to combat the common cold. Ingredients in the wax are different from those in the root, however, and the wax may cause severe irrita-tion internally.

Myrtle is symbolic of love according to the English language of flowers.

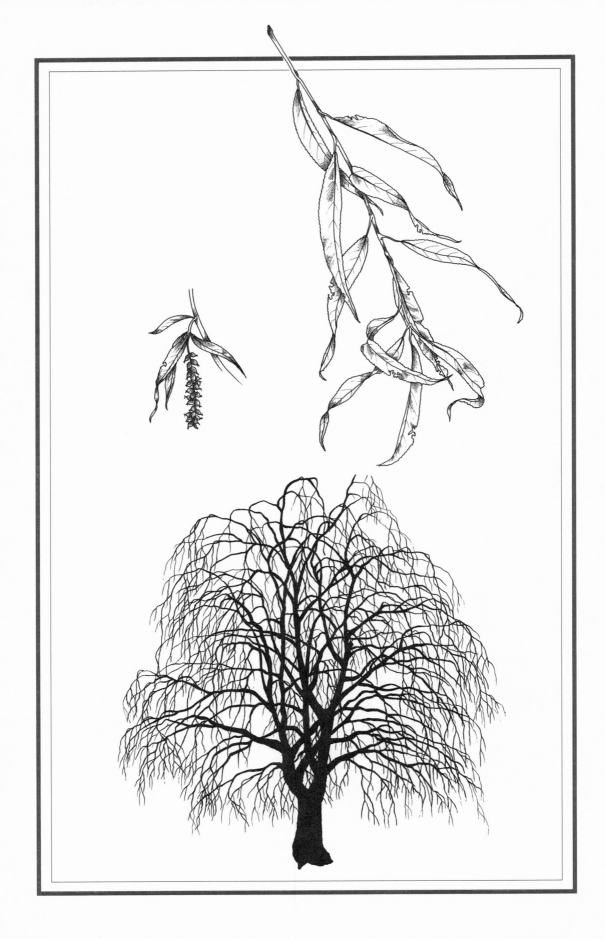

COMMON NAME: *Willow, Weeping*

BOTANICAL NAME: *Salix babylonica*

FAMILY: Salicaceae (Willow)

DESCRIPTION: Weeping willow has a graceful, drooping form. The leaves are narrow and lance-shaped, measuring 3 to 4 inches long. The tree reaches a height of about 70 feet and grows quickly. The flowers do not have petals or sepals but occur in clusters to form a catkin.

ORIGIN: Eurasia, northern Africa; naturalized in much of North America

HOW TO GROW: Willows grow in ordinary garden soil but also tolerate wet, poorly drained areas. They prefer damp areas and full sun and do particularly well planted along stream or river banks. It grows in zones 3 to 9.

There are more than 300 species of willows growing throughout the northern half of the world. The medicinal use of willow dates back to the first century A.D., when the Greek physician Dioscorides used a concoction made from willow bark to reduce pain and to break fever. Modern research has found that bark and leaves from willow are high in the chemical salicin, a substance closely resembling aspirin. Like aspirin of today, willow was used to treat everything from the common cold to rheumatism. It was often prescribed as an anti-inflammatory and a painkiller. Willow is no longer used medicinally because it causes unpleasant side effects such as stomach cramps and nausea.

Willows are useful in stabilizing stream and pond banks and in soil and water conservation. The roots of willow trees form mats, which are highly desirable for erosion control.

To the western pioneers, willows were always a welcomed sight, as they indicated that water was close by. Diaries, journals, and reports are full of happy exclamations of sighting willow trees.

Although willows are of only minor importance for their timber, willow wood is highly shock resistant, which makes it good for making artificial limbs, boxes, and woodenware. One species from England is particularly sought after for making cricket bats.

The valley willow, *S. nigra,* was used extensively by American Indians for a variety of purposes. Although the wood is weak and spindly and virtually useless as firewood, willow splints were woven into baskets that were so tight they could hold water. Willow is particularly useful for this purpose because when the wood gets wet it swells and tightens the baskets even further.

Honeybees are attracted to willows in spring and make delicious honey from the nectar.

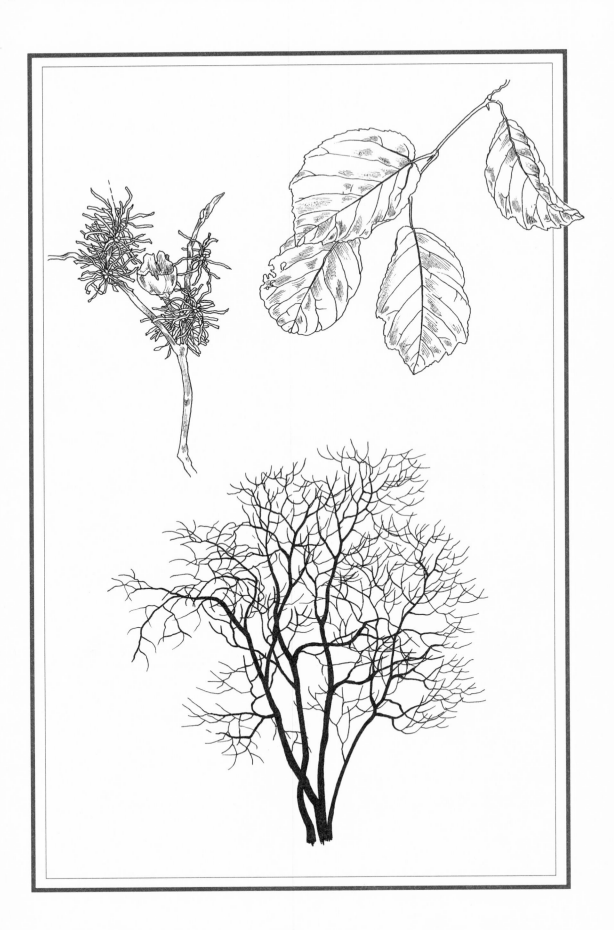

COMMON NAME: *Witch Hazel*

BOTANICAL NAME: *Hamamelis virginiana*

FAMILY: Hamamelidaceae (Witch hazel)

DESCRIPTION: Witch hazel is a lovely small tree of great ornamental value. It grows to a height of 20 to 30 feet with a trunk of 5 to 7 inches in diameter. The leaves are a dull dark green, lighter green underneath, and deeply veined, measuring 3 to 5 inches long. The attractive flowers are an inch wide and have four bright yellow slender petals. They occur on leafless branches in fall and winter. Many cultivars have been developed, all of which bear flowers that are either yellow or orange. The blossoms usually have a reddish tint toward the center. Some of the best cultivars include *H.* x intermedia 'Diane', which is a distinctly red color, and 'Jelena' which has dark yellow, brownish flowers.

ORIGIN: native throughout eastern United States

HOW TO GROW: Witch hazel should be planted in full sun or partial shade in soil that is neutral or slightly acidic. Most species of witch hazel are hardy to zone 5.

The name witch hazel was given to this small tree by English settlers who recognized it as being similar to many European species. The name witch refers not to magic and witchcraft, but to an old English word meaning "to bend." Another common name, snapping hazel, is so named because the seed pods burst open with such force that seeds are sometimes shot forth as far as 20 feet. European species of *Hamamelis* were sometimes used as divining rods to find water.

A common home remedy made from witch hazel bark, water, and alcohol has traditionally been used externally as an astringent to soothe sores and bruises. The tannins within the bark were also useful in eye medicines and in treating hemorrhoids.

Even today, tea made from the leaves is taken to relieve sore throats and colds. The leafy twigs are rubbed on athletes' legs to relieve muscle cramping. Although bottled witch-hazel water is available commercially, it is not as effective as the fresh witch-hazel water, as it does not contain the same astringent qualities that the fresh leaves do.

COMMON NAME: *Yew, English*
BOTANICAL NAME: *Taxus baccata*
FAMILY: Taxaceae (Yew)

DESCRIPTION: English yew is generally an upright shrub growing to heights of 3 to 6 feet and of similar width. The leaves are shiny needles with two light green lines on the undersides, and they are arranged in a flat plane along the branch. Many cultivars are available differing in height ('Prostrata' is a spreading plant growing only 3 to 6 inches high) and in foliage color ('Adpressa Aurea' has yellow needles). English yew is native to Europe, northern Africa, and western Asia. *T. cuspidata*, Japanese yew, has softer needles with yellow lines underneath. Cultivars range in height from 18 inches to 20 feet. It is native to Japan, Korea, and Manchuria. *T. brevifolia*, Pacific or western yew, grows about 50 feet tall and has flattened evergreen needles. The small brown seeds are enclosed in a bright scarlet-red cup. It is native from Montana west to British Columbia and California.

ORIGIN: See Description.

HOW TO GROW: Yews like full sun or partial shade and should be planted in rich, fertile acidic soil. The primary soil requirement is good drainage. Most yews benefit from frequent pruning and protection from drying winds and sun. English yew grows in zones 6 to 8 and should be planted 5 to 6 feet apart. Japanese yew grows in zones 5 to 8. Western yew grows in zones 6 to 8.

The species name *baccata* means "berrylike," which refers to the red-covered seed. *T. baccata* is one of the few evergreens native to Great Britain, thus the name English yew.

Yew is a relatively heavy wood for an evergreen. It produces a highly polished surface, a characteristic that makes it valuable as a veneer. In the past yew was much prized for creating archery bows. Today it is somewhat of a novelty, useful only as veneer, in cabinetry, or for making unusual furniture.

Almost all parts of yew are poisonous and, if consumed, may even be fatal. The exception to this is the red cup, which is thought to be edible and even tasty, as long as the toxic brown seed inside the cap is not eaten along with it.

Yew is a symbol of sorrow according to the English language of flowers.

COMMON NAME: *Yucca*

BOTANICAL NAME: *Yucca brevifolia*

FAMILY: Lilliaceae (Lily)

DESCRIPTION: The narrow-leaved ever-green tree has a short trunk with branches that reach skyward in often wildly grotesque forms. The thin, swordlike leaves are found in clusters, which spread fanlike at the ends. The tree reaches a height of 15 to 30 feet. Older, larger trunks are brown or gray and show deep furrows and cracks caused by aging. The flowers are bell-shaped and have six yellowish green sepals, occurring in dense clusters. They appear in spring and often smell somewhat like mushrooms. *Y. faxoniana*, Spanish bayonet, is a small evergreen tree having long bayonetlike leaves and stalks of bell-shaped white flowers. It is found on gravelly mountain slopes. *Y. filamentosa* is the species most often cultivated. It needs full sun and well-drained soil and is quite drought tolerant. The species has nearly 2½-foot-long leaves that taper to a sharp spine on the end. Leaf edges hold long, curly threads.

ORIGIN: Yucca is native to the Mojave desert in southwestern Utah, Nevada, California, and Arizona. It is usually found at elevations of 2,000 to 6,000 feet. In nature the trees are often found in groves.

HOW TO GROW: Joshua-tree and other yuccas like dry, well-drained soils.

The name yucca is from the Carib Indian word *yuca*, which actually refers to the root of cassava, an ancient name given to this plant.

Yucca is also known as yucca palm, yucca cactus, and Joshua yucca. *Y. brevifolia* was given the name Joshua-tree by Mormon pioneers who thought that the form of the tree looked like someone praying with arms uplifted, or perhaps like a person wildly gesturing. They named it after the prophet Joshua, as it reminded them of a figure pointing the way, perhaps to the promised land.

It is understandable that the Mormons believed that the yucca tree was leading them to the promised land because it seemed that everywhere they went they encountered this bizarre-looking tree. Although it has somewhat of an erratic distribution, it occurs repeatedly at certain elevations throughout Nevada and Utah.

Not everyone, however, sees the mystical beauty in Joshua-trees. Captain John C. Fremont called them the "most repulsive tree in the vegetable kingdom."

The age of the tree can be determined by the number of branches that develop annually. Some old trees boast up to one hundred branchlets.

Many parts of the tree were used by American Indians. The seeds were ground into meal, and a dye made from the red roots was used to decorate baskets. Because the wood is very strong in proportion to its weight, it was used for surgical splints

Wildlife, too, makes use of the tree. The now-extinct giant sloth ate the foliage. Red-shafted flickers drill holes in the tops of the branches. Once abandoned, the holes are used as nesting sites by other birds. Dead branches and leaves provide cover for the desert night-lizard. Woodrats use the spiny leaves for their nests.

Yucca flowers are pollinated by a small white moth, appropriately enough called the yucca moth. Both the flower and the moth benefit from a symbiotic relationship. The female moth gathers the pollen and pushes it into a tiny ball, then deposits it on the stigma of another flower. This serves to attract a multitude of insects, which obligingly pollinate the flower.

Once the ball is in place, the moth deposits her eggs. The small larvae feed off the growing fruit but always leave some seeds to mature.

American Indians ate the roasted fruits from the yucca tree. The fruits were also sometimes dried and then ground into meal.

The long daggerlike leaves from plants in this genus were made into fibers to make ropes, baskets, and mats.

Y. glauca, soapweed, was used by the American Indians to ease pain from sprains and broken bones. The root was crushed and made into a poultice for this purpose. It was also used by the Indians in steam baths and as a hair wash for dandruff and baldness.

In 1936 the United States government recognized the importance of this tree by establishing the Joshua Tree National Monument, found on 1,344 square miles of western desert.

SELECTED BIBLIOGRAPHY

Constantine, Albert, Jr. *Know Your Woods.* New York: Charles Scribner's Sons, 1959.

Cornell University. L.H. Bailey Hortorium. *Hortus Third.* New York: Arco Publishing Company, 1977.

Dewolf, Gordon P. *Taylor's Guide to Trees.* Revised edition of tree section of *Taylor's Encyclopedia of Gardening* by Norman Taylor. Boston: Houghton-Mifflin Company, 1988.

Dirr, Michael. *Manual of Woody Landscape Plants.* Champaign, Ill.: Stipes, 1990.

Dobelis, Inge N., ed. *Magic and Medicine of Plants.* Pleasantville, N.Y.: Reader's Digest Books, 1986.

Ewart, Neil. *The Lore of Flowers.* New York: Sterling Publishers, 1982.

Friend, Hilderic. *Flower Lore.* Rockport, Mass.: Para Research, 1981.

Greenaway, Kate. *The Illuminated Language of Flowers.* New York: Gramercy Publishing Company, 1978 (reprint of 1884 edition).

Haughton, Claire Shaver. *Green Immigrants: The Plants That Transformed America.* New York: Harcourt, Brace, Jovanovich, 1978.

Johnson, Hugh. *Hugh Johnson's Encyclopedia of Trees.* New York: Gallery Books, 1984.

Krussman, Gerd. *Manual of Cultivated Broad-leaved Trees and Shrubs,* Vol. 1-3. Portland, Oreg.: Timber Press, 1984.

—. *Manual of Cultivated Conifers.* Portland, Oreg.: Timber Press, 1985.

Little, Elbert L. *The Audubon Society Field Guide to North American Trees: Eastern Region.* New York: Alfred A. Knopf, 1980.

—. *The Audubon Society Field Guide to North American Trees: Western Region.* New York: Alfred A. Knopf, 1980.

Petrides, George A. *A Field Guide to Trees and Shrubs.* The Peterson Field Guide series. Boston: Houghton-Mifflin, Co., 1958.

Phillips, Roger and Martyn Rix. *Shrubs.* New York: Random House, 1989.

Rupp, Rebecca. *Red Oaks and Black Birches.* Pownal, Vt.: Garden Way Publishers, 1990.

Shosteck, Robert. *Flowers and Plants.* New York: The New York Times Book Company, 1974.

Stupka, Arthur. *Trees, Shrubs, and Woody Vines of Great Smoky Mountains National Park.* Knoxville: The University of Tennessee Press, 1964.

Sutton, Ann and Myron Sutton. *Eastern Forests.* The Audubon Society Nature Guides. New York: Alfred A. Knopf, n.d.

Thomson, William A.R., ed. *Medicines from the Earth: A Guide to Healing Plants.* San Francisco: Harper and Row, 1978.

Walker, Laurence C. *Trees.* Englewood Cliffs, N.J.: Prentice-Hall, 1984.

Wyman, Donald. *Shrubs for American Gardens.* New York: Macmillan, 1969.

—. *Trees for American Gardens.* New York: Macmillan, 1990.

Zucker, Isabel. *Flowering Shrubs and Small Trees.* New York: Grove Weidenfeld, 1990.

INDEX

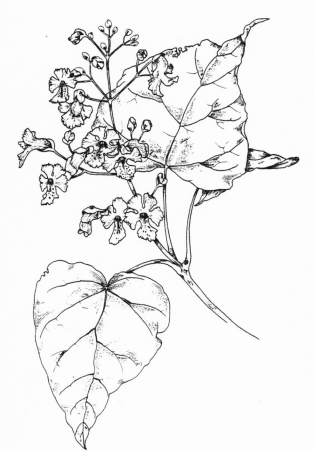

E

F

G

H

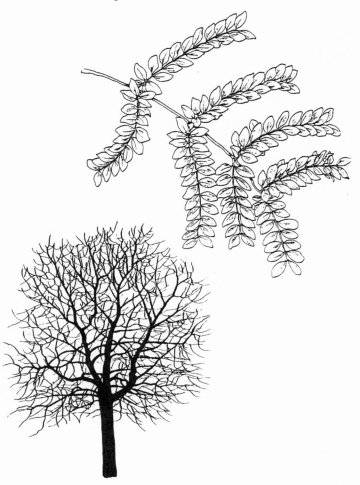

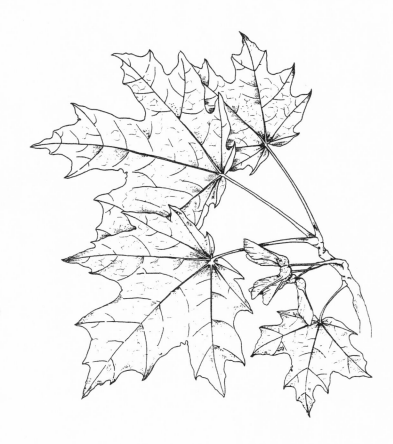

ABOUT THE AUTHOR

LAURA MARTIN lives in Atlanta, Georgia, with her two children, Cameron and David. She writes a weekly gardening column for the *Atlanta Journal-Constitution* and travels throughout the country lecturing on gardening. She is also the author of *Wildflower Folklore, Garden Flower Folklore,* and *The Wildflower Meadow Book,* published by The Globe Pequot Press, and *Southern Wildflowers* and *Grandmother's Garden,* published by Longstreet Press. In all of her work, Laura expresses great respect for the natural world and concern for environmental problems. As a board member for the Georgia Conservancy, she addresses these problems within her community.

Gardening

From lush picture books to no-nonsense practical manuals, here is a variety of beautifully produced titles on many aspects of gardening. Each of the gardening books listed is by an expert in his or her field and will provide hours of gardening enjoyment for expert and novice gardeners. Please check your local bookstore for other fine Globe Pequot Press titles, which include:

The Wildflower Meadow Book, $16.95

The National Trust Book of Wild Flower Gardening, $25.95

Garden Flower Folklore, $19.95

Wildflower Folklore, $23.95

Herbs, $19.95

Dahlias, $19.95

Rhododendrons, $19.95

Fuchsias, $19.95

Climbing Roses, $19.95

Modern Garden Roses, $19.95

Azaleas, $19.95

Auriculas, $19.95

Magnolias, $19.95

The Movable Garden, $15.95

Garden Smarts, $12.95

To order any of these titles with MASTERCARD or VISA call toll-free 1-800-243-0495; in Connecticut call 1-800-962-0973. Free shipping for orders of three or more books. Shipping charge of $3.00 per book for one or two books ordered. Connecticut residents add sales tax. Ask for your free catalogue of Globe Pequot's quality books on recreation, travel, nature, gardening, cooking, crafts, and more. Prices and availability subject to change.